A ROAD BACK FROM
SCHIZOPHRENIA

A ROAD BACK FROM SCHIZOPHRENIA

A Memoir
Arnhild Lauveng
Translated by Stine Skarpnes Østtveit

Skyhorse Publishing, Inc.
New York

Library of Congress Cataloging-in-Publication Data
Lauveng, Arnhild.
[I morgen var jeg alltid en løve. English]
A road back from schizophrenia : a memoir / Arnhild Lauveng ; translated by Stine Skarpnes Østtveit.
    p. ; cm.
Includes bibliographical references.
ISBN 978-1-61608-871-2 (hardcover : alk. paper)
I. Title.
[DNLM: 1. Lauveng, Arnhild. 2. Schizophrenia--Autobiography. 3. Hospitalization--Autobiography. 4. Mentally Ill Persons--Autobiography. 5. Schizophrenia--therapy. WM 40]
616.89'80092--dc23
 [B]

2012035423

Paperback ISBN: 978-1-5107-2495-2

Printed in the United States of America

I used to live my days like a sheep

Every day the shepherds would gather all of us at the ward and
lead us in a common march
And as most shepherd dogs they barked irritably if any of us
hesitated to walk through the door
Sometimes I would bleat, just a little, silently,
As they herded me through the halls,
But no one ever asked me why
—when you are crazy, you can bleat if you want

I used to live my days like a sheep
In a common herd they would guide us through the hallways of
the hospital,
A slow, diverse herd of sheep that no one thought to see.
Because we were a herd,
And the whole herd was walking,
And the whole herd was locked back up.

I used to live my days like a sheep
The shepherds cut my wool and shaved my claws
So that I would fit in the herd better.
I walked among prettily groomed donkeys, bears, squirrels, and
crocodiles
And wondered why nobody wanted to see

I used to live my days like a sheep
While I dreamed of hunting across the Savannahs
And I let myself drift from fields to fencing to barns
When they said that was the best way for a sheep.
And I knew it was wrong.
And I knew that it wouldn't last forever.

For I lived my days as a sheep.
But tomorrow I was always a lion.

Contents

Foreword

The reason I am writing this book is that I am a former schizophrenic. This sounds just as impossible as "former AIDS patient" or "former diabetic." A former schizophrenic is something that basically doesn't exist. It is a role that is never offered. You may be a misdiagnosed schizophrenic. You are also allowed to be a symptom-free schizophrenic, who is able to keep the sickness in check with medical aids, or you can be a schizophrenic who manages to live with your symptoms or is just going through a good period. There is nothing wrong with these alternatives, but they are not true to my situation. I have been schizophrenic. I know how it was. I know how the world looked then, how it was perceived, what I was thinking, and what I had to do. I have also experienced "good periods." I know how these felt. And I know how things are now. This is something completely different. Now, I am healthy. That label needs to be allowed as well.

It is not easy to estimate exactly how long I was sick because it took years to slowly glide into the decease, and it took years to crawl out again. I suffered from suicidal thoughts and distorted senses for years before anyone knew that I was becoming a schizophrenic. And I had gained much healthiness, safety, and insight long before the system officially realized that I would be free of the disease. Both sickness and healthiness are processes and levels and cannot really be given a set time frame. However, I first started to be sick as early as fourteen or fifteen years old. When I was seventeen, I was admitted for the first time. After that, it was back and forth, in and out, with shorter and longer stays for years. The shortest hospitalizations would just be a couple of days or weeks at the ER; other admissions would last for months; and the longest lasted for one to two years at closed or open wards, voluntary or by force. Altogether, I was hospitalized for between six and seven years. The last time I was admitted, I was twenty-six years old, but at that time I was getting better, even though it might not have been as apparent to others as it was to me.

I don't believe that my story is anything more than my own story. It may not be true for everyone. But it is a different story than what people first diagnosed with schizophrenia may be told; therefore, I find it important to share. When I was sick, doctors told me only one story. They said that I was sick, that it was something I was born with, that it would last for my entire life, and that I would have to learn how to live with it. This was not a story that suited me. This was not a story that gave me courage and strength and hope at a time when I more than ever before needed courage and strength and hope. It was not a story that did me any good. And, in my case, nor was it a true story. But it was the only story I received.

After becoming healthy, I became a psychologist. This education has shown me that even if I overlook my private story, and myself, there are many other stories to share with people diagnosed with schizophrenia and the people that work and live with them. So, I will share a couple more, and some of my own. These stories may not be fitting for everyone. Life is large and complicated and intricate, and there are no universal answers. Universal answers are for math, not for real life. In other words, none of these stories represent the one, large, common Truth. But all the stories are true.

STORIES OF CONFUSION

Fog, dragons, blood, and iron

It started carefully and gradually, and I almost didn't notice. It was like a nice summer day when the fog slowly creeps over the sky. First as a thin veil over the sun, then gradually more, but the sun is still shining, and not until it stops, when it suddenly gets cold and the birds have stopped chirping, do you realize what is happening. But by then the fog is already there, the sun is gone, landmarks are starting to disappear, and you don't have time to find your way home because the fog is so heavy that all the roads are gone. And then the fear hits you. Because you don't know what happened, or why, or how long it will last, but you understand that you are alone and that you are lost and you are scared that you may never find the way back home.

I am not sure when it first began, or how it first began, but I remember that I first started to be scared in middle school. There wasn't much to be scared of yet, and I wasn't very scared either, but I did notice that something wasn't right. I had always been the nice, quiet, good girl that kept to herself, daydreamed a lot, and didn't have many friends. I had some, especially one I was very close to—a good best friend—but we were never a large group. In elementary school I was bullied a lot. It wasn't violent in any way,

3

but rather it was a quiet and calm everyday teasing that is almost invisible, but steals confidence and friendship and laughter, and leaves you by yourself, confident that being alone is the best solution for you. There was bullying at middle school as well—not much, but enough. Bubble gum in my hair, kids leaving when I entered a room, people pulling away their chairs and laughing mockingly. Group work was a nightmare, and I kept to myself during recess. It had been this way for a long time, but suddenly I started to realize that I was more alone than before, and it was no longer just an external loneliness, but it started growing inside of me as well. At one point something happened; I was no longer alone because I did not have anyone to be with, but rather because the fog made it hard to communicate, and the loneliness had become part of me.

I got good grades in school. I spent time with my best friend, went to the movies, babysat, drew, painted, and listened to music. I laughed; I had many plans for my future. But I started going out more at night, taking long walks where I thought of everything and nothing, and sometimes I didn't even know where I had been by the time I got back. I thought a lot about death, and I climbed to the top of the ski jumping hill in the middle of summer and thought about how it would be to jump and fly downward and land in a completely different place, the place you don't return from. I think I killed someone in every single essay I wrote all though middle school, maybe with the exception of nonfiction essays, but they, too, were pretty gloomy. I quieted down and started listening to music a lot. I spent a lot of time reading, most often sad and heavy books, maybe too heavy for a fourteen-year-old. *The Bleaching Yard* and *The Birds* by Tarjei Vesaas; Kafka and Dostoevsky. I became very grown-up and very childish, and I basically lost track of who I was. When I was in ninth grade, for Christmas I wished for a Latin textbook and a baby doll. I was increasingly confused and I wrote a lot, and pensively, in my diary.

But none of these things are really that out of the ordinary. I was a teenager, and teenagers are usually unpredictable. They are torn between being a young child and being somewhat grown-up, and much thought and sudden mood swings are really very normal and nothing to worry about. Upon reflection years later, I think the main warning signal was my identity—the safety of knowing that I was an "I"—was starting to crumble. I became increasingly insecure about whether or not I really existed, or if I was only a character in a book or a being someone had made up. I was no longer certain of who was controlling my thoughts and actions; was it me, or was it someone else—the author may-be? I started feeling insecure about whether or not I was alive, really alive, because everything felt so empty and gray. In my diary I replaced "I" with "she" and after a while I started think-ing like this as well: "She was walking to school. She was sad and wondering if she was going to die." And someplace within me, something was questioning if "she" was still "me," and it found out that *that* was impossible, because "she" was sad, and I, well, I was nothing. Just gray.

It was around this time that I realized that I needed help. I dreaded it for a long time, but one day, when I was sitting by my-self in a classroom to finish some homework, I decided to visit the health nurse. She was sweet and nice, but I didn't feel like I was able to explain myself properly. She asked if I ate, and I did, and if I was afraid to gain weight or to drive a car, but I was nei-ther. I was afraid of not existing, and I was afraid of my thoughts not being my own, but she didn't ask about that. I said that every-thing felt gray and that I just couldn't bear living anymore, and at that time she set up an appointment for me with the school psychologist. I was scared and embarrassed, and I didn't want to tell anyone. The appointment was during winter break, so the school was luckily closed.

At home, I told my parents that I was going for a walk, and then I hid out in the cemetery, right by the school, until I saw the school psychologist walk in. I really did want to talk with him, even though I was scared, because I understood that I was losing my way in the fog, and I needed help. But I didn't know how to ask for it or explain what was happening, because the fog was already quite thick and it had become difficult to communicate. I told him that I was confused, and he responded that this was common among teens. I said that I felt like I wasn't in charge of my feelings or actions anymore. He then drew Freudian circles for me with an "id" and "ego" and "super ego." I didn't understand this at all, but it made me quite sure that *he* didn't understand anything of what I was trying to say. My next appointment with him interfered with a test, so I ran down to the nurse and said that I didn't have time and that I didn't need the appointment anyway because I was feeling better. This was a straight-out lie, but the fog was really thick now, and it became increasingly hard to form reasonable thoughts and even harder to talk about them, so the lie was just easier. I knew that I would never be able to express how it really was. So I said that everything was fine and whirred on by myself.

Strangely enough, I was still keeping up with my schoolwork. My essays were tragic but still well written, and my science and math classes went fine. Dates and kings and wars and chemical formulas were safe, simple, and firm facts in a world that was increasingly chaotic, and they gave me no trouble. They were what they were, insensitive and unchangeable and completely unaffected by my chaos; they could be memorized and studied and all was fine. I went on walks, babysat, did my homework, and took tests, and nobody knew that each day I was getting more lost and was drifting further away from home. But I did.

And then I started high school. In the beginning it was fine. I was placed in a nice class, with some of the people I knew from before and many fresh faces, and I discovered that people could be nice and that I could get more friends and that I could have fun with them. I got a job next to the school, as a chocolate saleswoman at a movie theater in the city, and even if the bus ride was long, I was happy with both the job and my colleagues. I was feeling good. Very good. Too good. Because this wasn't the world I was used to, and when things got that good, it became even more apparent how painful and lonely it had been before. And the sorrow I was carrying was still there, and when I laughed with the others, the sorrow would twist and turn and remind me that life wasn't this easy and fun, but lonely, cruel, and sad. And so I felt even more alone. Furthermore, I had been bullied for so long that it felt tiresome and uncomfortable that people were suddenly nice to me. And if I were to accept that they actually *were* nice, and that it wasn't an inevitability that they wouldn't be, well, then, I would also have to accept the sorrow of what had been before. That I couldn't handle. And the grayness grew. It became increasingly clear that I was uncomfortable in the role of quiet, nice, and good girl. I wanted to fly, and I started drawing golden-red, fire-breathing dragons, dragons that glowed with power and life and everything I didn't have. Because I was only gray.

In middle school my senses already had started to change a bit. This, too, happened so slowly and carefully that I almost didn't notice at first, but sometimes, especially when I was tired, noises sounded strange. They were sometimes too high, or too low, or just strange. Now, it grew worse. Usually there is a clear order when it comes to sound—some are high, some low, some important, and some less important—but now many of these rules were unclear. I might be walking and talking with people and find that it was hard to hear what they were saying, because their voices were overpowered by the sound of my sneakers hitting the asphalt. The hissing in pipes could get loud and threatening and physically painful, and sometimes I was unsure of what the sound really was; was it just hissing or was someone talking? In the same way, my teacher's lectures would lose words and content and become sounds, like the whining of a saw blade or the howling wind.

What I saw was changing as well; the distinctions between light and shadow became more apparent and, at times, quite scary. When I was walking down the street, the houses around me could grow large and threatening, or I felt like they were falling toward me. Familiar rules of perspective blurred, and it was like walking around in a surrealistic painting by Picasso or Salvador Dali—both tiresome and confusing. One day, on my way to work, I ended up glued to the ground for half an hour, not daring to cross the street. I was unable to judge the distance to the cars, and the edge of the curb seemed like a bottomless cliff that would kill me if I fell off it. This anxiety and despair grew, and at the end of it, I saw no other way out than to just walk. If I was killed, then at least it was over. I wasn't killed. I crossed the street, found my way to work, and said that the bus was late. That was the first time I was late for work, and it was fine, but I felt horrible for lying. But at the same time, what was I supposed to say? That I had been afraid I would kill myself if I fell from the curb? That was just not possible. It would sound insane. While the world was becoming messier, there was still something inside of me that registered what was happening and understood that it was wrong. I *knew*, on some level, that curbs are 6 to 8 inches high, not 50 to 65 feet, and that you don't *die* when you step down from one; but it didn't look that way, and even though one part of me said one thing, another part said something completely different, and it became increasingly harder to understand and make sense of these things.

I continued to write my diary, and I still wrote about "she." This confused me. If I was "she," then who was writing *about* "she"? Am "I" "she"? But if "I" am "she," then who is telling the story about "I" and "she"? It got more and more chaotic, and I couldn't work it out. One night I gave up on the whole thing and replaced every "I" with an *x*, for unknown. I felt like I had ceased to exist; everything was a mess; I had no idea if I was or who or what I was. I just wasn't anymore; I wasn't a person with an identity or boundaries or a beginning and an end. I was an indefinable and fluid chaos, like a cloud of fog, woolly and without limits. But *I* was still me. When I now read my diary from the night I felt like my identity dissolved completely and the psychosis took over, I can see it. Because then, when the chaos threatened and I was in such despair that I couldn't handle it anymore, I wrote, in direct quotes, "Now x can handle no more. X has no idea who x is and just can't think about it anymore either. X thinks x will put y (3rd singular person) to bed." And even though I clearly remember the despair and loneliness in being completely and utterly alone, without even a solid "I," I still have to smile. Because it becomes so evident that I was there all along, and that the identity was solid even though the experience of it had crumbled away. I *am* interested in grammar and language; that is one of the traits and unique qualities that creates my identity and make me who I am. So I was there back then as well. I just didn't see it.

The world had turned gray, my senses were a mess, and I didn't know how to relate to the conflict between "good girl" and "living life." My role was so narrow that my soul was blistered; it ached all the time, but I had no idea how to move on. I drew dragons—individual drawings of golden creatures that flew through the night, and series containing multiple pictures that together made a whole story. One of these series started with an ice princess in a blue-purple dress who was walking alone though a dark winter forest with naked, dead trees. The forest was filled with wild animals—wolves, snakes, little devils—but none of them saw the ice princess; they all just turned and walked in the opposite direction. She was completely and utterly alone. In the next picture the princess was swallowed by the large, golden, fire-breathing dragon, which actually looked nice, even when he ate the princess. The third picture showed the dragon brooding on a large, white egg, and in the fourth picture the egg cracks and a golden-red princess came out. Both she and the dragon smiled happily. In the very last picture the fire princess walked through the woods once more. The forest was just as dark and cold, and just as full of wild and dangerous animals. But the princess didn't fit in anymore, and the animals could tell, and in this photo all of the animals walked toward her and attacked her. The ice no longer protected her; she was now alone and vulnerable and may have been in danger of being eaten. Despite this, I wrote in my journal: "It doesn't matter what it costs, I will not die before I have painted with all the colors in my paint box, I will not live in pastel colors." And I wrote this, even though I, not knowing anything about the future, had drawn an unnervingly accurate photo of what would happen. I knew I was about to be swallowed, and I knew that I would survive.

In another drawing series, the ice princess is about to be swallowed by a flock of small wool chunks without bodies, but with large mouths. To escape, she decides to yet again let the dragon swallow her. This time the dragon doesn't lay an egg, but it is lying in a meadow, crying. The tears gather and form a river, and by the riverbank a flower grows. The bud cracks and the fire princess comes out, singing.

I was completely confused, I understood nothing, and I couldn't explain what was happening to me, because I didn't know myself. I remember it and I know that it is true. But the drawings, nicely dated from the beginning, still tell the entire story. They show that I knew nothing, yet understood everything.

There were other areas wherein I expressed the things I could not put words to as well. I did not feel comfortable in my role, but instead of dropping it, I became great at it. I worked every day after school, but I still wanted just as good, or better, grades. I studied at night after I came home from work and long into the night hours. Then I got a few hours' sleep, before I got up at the crack of dawn, studied some more or did chores, silently so no one noticed me, then went back to school again, and then to work, followed by more homework. There was no time for friends or hobbies, and even though that was unfortunate, it was safe because then I didn't have to mourn my lonely years. Everything had just as bad as it had always been, and that wasn't good, but at least it was familiar.

I slept less and started to eat less, not because I was trying to lose weight, but because I wanted to push myself and be in control of the chaos. Then the Captain came. The first time I met him, I was writing in my diary. I was tired and I was sitting down and writing, and I suddenly realized that one of the sentences ended in a different way than I had wanted. This frightened me, and I wrote, "Who finished that sentence?" And he said: "I did," and so it began. The road from writing to thoughts and finally voices is very short; at least it was for me. My senses had been confused and distorted for a while, and the step to hearing voices was therefore not very large. I guess I had heard it before this point as well, or been unsure of what I heard, but the voices had been unclear; mumbling, distant noise, a sound like talking—but I was unable to catch the words or who was talking. At this point, there was no doubt. It was the Captain who was talking, and he was speaking clearly. It was impossible to misunderstand him. The Captain was captain, and captains give orders. But he was kind as well, at least in the beginning. He was pleasant and said that he would take care of me, that I didn't have to worry about anyone else because he would be there for me. He said that nobody knew me as well as he did, and he gave me proof by telling me about my dreams and aspirations, which was quite easy considering he was me. He said that I no longer had to think about whether or not other people liked me, and that I no longer needed to worry about what I wanted or who I should be. He would take care of all of that. And he promised to never leave me. I just had to trust him and do as he said. And I did. It wasn't that hard to begin with. "You should work on that assignment some more," the Captain said. And I wrote the assignment over. "It is still not good enough," the Captain said. "Trust me, it's not good, write it one more time!" I trusted him. And I wrote the assignment over once more, found new facts, and polished the outline. "Not good," said the Captain. "You must be stupid, but you are still lucky to have me to help you. Write it again, and right this time!"

But I couldn't, because I was so tired, and it was almost 4 a.m., and it was just a common assignment that I had already written three times, and it wasn't necessary to work this hard on it. "Not only stupid, but lazy as well," the Captain said. Then he hit my face hard, multiple times, so that I would learn to behave properly and so that I wouldn't break completely. I knew—I saw—that it was my own hand hitting me, but it felt like someone else was steering my hand. It may sound strange, but at this point I had doubted who was controlling my thoughts and my actions for several years, and I wasn't even sure that I existed at all, and therefore this was the next step, to lose control over my hands—a small step really. I was ready and worked, so when the Captain hit me, my experience was that he was the one doing the beating. I was scared, and I couldn't stop him. He hit me hard, while screaming insults in my head, louder and louder. And then he would quiet down a bit. I dried my tears and wrote the assignment one more time. It was still not good, but I managed to improve it, and now it was the morning and I had to get to school. The Captain walked me to school, and he was just nice enough that I was grateful that he was so nice to me and looked after me so that I didn't do anything stupid.

After that time, he hit me often—every time I did something wrong. And he often thought that I did something wrong. I was too late, too stupid, and too lazy. If I dawdled with making change while working at the movie theater kiosk, he would take me to the bathroom during my break and hit me in the face, multiple times. If I forgot a textbook or was sloppy with a homework assignment, he would hit me again. He would make me bring a stick or rod when I walked or bicycled to school, and he would hit me with it over the legs if I moved too slowly. I hated it, because it was so embarrassing, not to mention the fact that it hurt. I would always be slapped when we were alone, or when he had made sure that we were alone, but he would use the stick when I walked or bicycled outside, where others could see. Furthermore, the stick left marks; the slaps didn't. And the marks weren't easy to explain. I was very aware that I had hit myself, but I felt like it was beyond my control. It was the Captain hitting me but with my hands, and I knew and experienced this, but I couldn't explain it because it was a reality I lacked words to explain. As a result, I said as little as possible.

The Captain thought I was exceptionally lazy. He thought I slept too much and that I ate too much. So he started setting new demands. Twenty-five hours of sleep in a week was enough, he said. Later, he decreased it to twenty. If I didn't do as he said, he would hit me and reprimand me. He said that one meal a day was enough. That was more than enough. Actually too much, he found after a while, and he lowered the rations to three meals a week. I tried to create a system and find out which days I needed food the most. But he was still kind now and then, and I still believed him when he said it was for my own good.

Now I heard him almost all the time, and I could still hear other voices from time to time, voices that weren't as clear but still clearer than before. From the very beginning the Captain had talked about a "we," and I understood that there were more of them, with him as the leader. The Captain gave me a secret name, a name that was for their use only, and he said that the name made me one of them. He told me about a land with forests and iron where the trees had leaves that were blood red. Blood and iron. Pure power. Just what I longed for. But in order to get there, I first needed to show that I was worthy, and not such a pathetic coward. This I could understand; I was absolutely not sure that I was worthy. I was actually more or less sure that I wasn't and I was glad that the Captain would help me. Even if it did hurt when he hit me.

One day on my way home from school, tired and fed up and carrying a heavy backpack through the November slush, I saw a woman standing by the mailboxes outside my house. She had dark hair up in a bun and a simple, soft dress, which was solid white and solid navy at the same time. She was beautiful, and she smiled. It felt good to have someone smiling at me, so I smiled back. My day at school had been awful with group work and group discussions, and it was very hard to perform in groups with other students when I, first and foremost, had to cooperate with the Captain at all times. For that reason, the group work went badly, the Captain was infuriated, and I was simply exhausted. I needed a smile, and I was glad that she smiled at me—also because it was from her in particular. I had never seen her before, but I knew who she was. She was Loneliness, and she was beautiful. Who needed a group when Loneliness was so fine? After that day I saw her often. She didn't say much, but she had a beautiful and slightly sad smile. And at times she danced for me, in her beautiful dress, solid white and solid navy at the same time.

Soon I saw the Captain as well. Not every time I heard him, and not very clearly, but enough that I knew how he looked. It wasn't frightening really. I had heard his voice for so long, and it wasn't much of an adjustment to see him as well. It was around this time that I also started seeing wolves in the hallways at school. Wolves and crocodiles. They frightened me, because they looked angry, and they frightened me because nobody else could see them. I longed to get away from this mess, but I had yet to be found worthy to enter the land with the red forests. I started wondering if the best solution would be to die; that would be a way to escape at least. And I really needed to get away.

My mother obviously didn't see the wolves, and she couldn't hear the Captain. But she saw that I was eating less and less and that I refused to eat more, even if she tried to force me. She saw that I was turning pale and skinny, and even though she might not have been aware of how little I actually slept, she knew that I wasn't sleeping enough. She set up an appointment for me with my doctor, and even though I felt stupid, I knew that I needed help. But I was unable to say what was wrong. To me, it was impossible to describe what was going on. I talked to the doctor a few times. I was unable to explain what was going on properly, or what my world had become, but I still enjoyed talking to him. He seemed friendly. Yet, I was terrified when he said that he wanted to refer me to the children and youth psychiatry department. I told him that I had talked to the school psychologist and that it wasn't helpful, and he said that this was different, more advanced. This scared me even more, because I didn't feel advanced at all. Just small, stupid, and scared.

He gave me a referral, and I made an appointment, and that was okay. Good, actually. I liked my therapist, and it was important, because my world was now falling to pieces. Hiding things had been fine for a while, but now all the layers were cracking open and revealing that my world was complete chaos where nothing made sense. I desperately longed for blood, fire, and dragons, but I lived in a fog that continuously thickened. So I started to scratch myself till I bled to make sure that there was still living blood in my veins. My ability to communicate with the Captain and the others was diminishing, and my senses were no longer trustworthy, so I went down to the girls' bathroom and fought the Captain and wolves. I hit my face, bit my hands, and knocked my head against the wall to make the voices stop. Despite the fact that I chose the bathroom that was furthest away from everyone else, I was eventually discovered. The good student had gone completely mad, and my senses were so disturbed that I couldn't register that the teachers' looks had changed from appreciative to compassionate. My grades for the first semester were at the top of my class. By summer, though, I was flunking all my classes.

Still, I went back to school the following fall, despite a summer that had just made everything worse. I had many absences during the year, and even when I was there, my mind wasn't really there, and I couldn't keep up. A warm day in August I went for a long bike ride. I was at the cemetery and talked to my dad, and I visited other cemeteries. Then I rode my bike home. Despite the heat I was wearing a pink cotton sweater and light blue jeans. Pastel colors. And not very nice looking. I walked into the living room where my mother was sitting and said that I was ready. I now wanted to enter the forest. "Can't you see that I'm wearing the red dress?" I said. But my mother didn't see the red dress. She saw jeans and a pink sweater. "No," I said, and sat down by the window. "I have my red dress on now, and I am ready, they'll come to get me soon." My mother was understandably frightened and called my therapist, who came to our house. I thought it was nice to see her, but I had no need to talk to her. "It's over now," I said. "Thank you for your help, but now I will go to the forest. They'll come get me soon."

And they did. A short while after, I was picked up by the police and a doctor and brought to a closed ward. But it was too late. I had already disappeared into the forest. It was a dense forest, and it took me years to come back out.

Loneliness in a blue-white dress

Loneliness was a slender, dark woman with a long dress both solid white and solid navy at the same time. I have never managed to draw this or even explain it properly. The closest I can manage is a shadow on a wall. You can see the white color of the wall, while at the same time the blue-gray shadow—both at the same time. Loneliness came to visit often; she was as real to me as the Captain. And now, after all this time has passed, I think the image is quite beautiful and it nicely describes how it feels to be a slightly weird and dreaming and independent and lonely teenager. It is virginal, clean, and white-and-blue Monday blues. Both parts fully represented. And at the same time.

I also think I now know where she came from. I didn't see it then, but when I think of how she looked, I now recognize her. She looks like one of my ballet teachers. When I was little, I danced classical ballet for many years. I was never any good, but I liked dancing, and I always wished for dancing lessons for Christmas and for birthdays. At most, I danced three times a week. My first ballet teacher was Marie. She was small and elegant like a wagtail, with dark hair in a tight bun. She was quiet, dark, and skinny, but also very kind and with a strength of her own in her small body. She always wore a dark-blue ballet tricot with a dark-blue dancing skirt over it, and it was impossible to imagine her anywhere else then in a ballet hall or on a stage. She was a dancer, and as a child I thought she was absolutely fabulous, and I wanted to be like her. When I started taking more classes, the times didn't always match Marie's classes, and I had another teacher some nights. Her name was Mathilde and she was a bubbly, lively power center much larger than Marie, with a very different, but just as rare, elegance. Mathilde would laugh a lot during lessons and wore different ballet clothes in bright colors and patterns all the time. We used slightly different music in class but were worked just as hard, and we learned just as much, but in a different way. Mathilde became pregnant, but she still continued to dance up until the end of her pregnancy; she just stopped showing us jumps, and a short while after the baby was born, she was just as fit and powerful, with the baby in a basket next to the record player. Marie was the ethereal elegance. Mathilde was the powerful life. Marie danced ballet after Russian traditions, and Mathilde danced after the English. I danced three times a week and had for a long time, and eventually I started to get better. The management of the school said that I could start dancing en pointe next semester, and they recommended that I choose one direction, Russian or English, in order to specialize. I had looked forward to getting pointe shoes for a long time, and I was glad that I was finally ready, but I had no idea how I would ever choose between the two traditions. I said that I would think about it and get back to them. The last classes of the semester I was sick, and during Christmas break I told my mom that dance took too much time away from school and that I had no intention of becoming a professional dancer anyway—that I had gotten too old to have the energy to dance so often. And then I quit.

Without my knowledge, the manager of the school had hit one of my most basic weak points: kind, good, quiet, and ethereal; or lively, vibrant, and colorful. The choice wasn't really about choosing a ballet teacher but about choosing who I wanted to be, whom I wanted to identify with. And even though I wanted to identify with Mathilde, I would have thought this a betrayal of myself and Marie; besides, I didn't know if it was possible for me to be that lively. It might be that I really belonged in Marie's world. And even though none of these thoughts were conscious or clear back then, and even though I didn't have the ability to express it clearly, there was definitely something within me that made it impossible to make a choice.

So I chose not to choose. And a few years later, when I faced the same conflict again, with tight roles and the choice between glowing life desire and the cool good girl, Marie returned to me. Depressive navy and angelic white. At the same time. I saw her, but I couldn't see what she was saying. And nobody but me could hear her, either.

In actuality I *saw* many things; I had many sight illusions, which is really not that common when you have schizophrenia. I don't know why it happened that way for me, but I know that it has always been easy for me to picture things. I have a good visual memory, and I often picture things to find solutions to all kinds of daily problems. In that way, it seems natural that sight was a tool I could use to express feelings and knowledge that there were no words to describe. Because it is not like all of the hallucinations were something that I created externally and that they had nothing to do with the person itself. Quite the opposite. No matter what you think—and believe me—when you are sick, the hallucinations and other symptoms come from within and are created out of one's own interests and life.

For a period of time I stayed at a youth ward with many teenage boys. They saw a lot of aliens, martians, surveillance equipment, and espionage conspiracies a la James Bond. That suited them. I saw a lot of animals. Wolves, snakes, rats, large raptors. That's not surprising. I could have never created aliens. They don't really interest me, and I know little about them. But I am interested in animals, and even though it's doubtful that my visions were biologically correct (like two-foot long rats and orange and purple crocodiles), I know enough about animals and animal life that I have a relationship to it and can be creative with it. And this is necessary in order to create a hallucination, even when one is not conscious that one is creating the visions on one's own. Because that was never clear.

Wolves bothered me most. Large, scary wolves, with yellow eyes, ragged fur, bad hot breath, and grinding teeth. I saw them often—they showed up in school, in the classroom; they were at the various hospitals I was sent to (both the closed and the open wards); they were at the bus and at the mall. There were wolves everywhere. I lived in a wolf hall. I could see them, hear their snarling, and sometimes I could even smell them. This confused me, because in reality I knew that there couldn't possibly be wolves everywhere. The high school I went to was situated in the middle of Lørenskog, between highways and shopping malls—there couldn't be wolves there! And inside the hospital wards—I was very well aware of how closed and locked they were, and how impossible it was to get in and out—there *couldn't* be wolves. And yet I saw them. And what was I to believe? We sometimes say, "I don't believe my own eyes"—but we do—even when what we see is very surprising. We are used to trusting our eyes, and our ears, and we are used to counting on the facts that are supposed to be real. So, what is one to do when one sees something that one knows, deep down, cannot be real?

I knew little of psychology, and even less about neuropsychology and the neuropsychological functions connected to perception and interpreting of sensations. I was unaware that when you picture something—picture images or situations—you use the exact same sight channels as when you actually see something in the external world. I was seventeen years old and knew that people who saw things that weren't really there were "crazy." All I knew about being crazy I had learned from American movies and books like *One Flew Over the Cuckoo's Nest* and *I Never Promised You a Rose Garden*. And books like these had convinced me that I absolutely did not want to be crazy. I didn't feel crazy, either. I was confused, scared, and unhappy, but I was still me, and, personally, I didn't feel mad. Consequently, the most logical solution was to assume that the things I saw really did exist and to trust the fact that the wolves existed too. That they were real. Even though I did find it a little odd deep down, nobody ever managed to convince me differently, no matter how hard they argued. It wasn't that I didn't agree with their arguments, because I did; it was just that accepting their point of view meant paying a high cost.

There was one other reason why I couldn't agree that the wolves—and all the other things I saw and heard—were "hallucinations," and that was a feeling I had that they were important somehow. After it became clear to everyone else that I was sick, and after I had met with a psychologist for a while and ultimately admitted to the hospital, people would repeatedly tell me that I was sick and that my sickness was the reason I saw these things. The wolves became a symptom, something unwanted and unimportant, like a cough or a rash—something that should be removed. It became an injury, a weakness, a result of how the brain was wired wrong because of genetic defects, or a traumatic childhood, or both. And this explanation did not go with what I knew. Because without being able to explain it, and without being able to give a reason for it, I knew that the wolves were not a mistake. Neither were any of the other things I saw or heard. They were important and absolute truths, expressed in a somewhat clumsy way, kind of like dreams. And just like dreams, they also needed to be interpreted in order to give meaning. But in order to interpret them, I first needed to be clear that they were true and real, even though it was a metaphoric truth and not a literal one.

After I had been diagnosed as sick, I stayed in the psychological ward for a while. That was around the time I started to get better, even though I didn't realize it yet. Because I had quit my studies when I first got sick, I was now taking classes through adult learning lessons, and it went quite well. Until I started English class. I was never good at English. I understand a decent amount of it, but my pronunciation is awful and my spelling even worse. So I tried for a while, and then I quit. Everybody thought this was fine. After all, I was chronically schizophrenic, confused, self-injurious, and hallucinated, and it was no huge surprise that I couldn't graduate. But some of the other patients at the hospital encouraged me. By chance, the brother of my English teacher was also admitted to the same ward as me, and with the help of another amazing girl at the hospital, I was convinced that I should give English another try. But I didn't tell anyone. I didn't want anyone to expect anything, and I didn't want anyone to ask me how it was going if I didn't wish to share. So I studied in my room and didn't go to lectures, and one night I said I was going on a bike ride. I biked over to the school, finally received a syllabus and an invoice for the exam fee, and no one but the teacher knew anything about it at all.

On my way home from the school, large rats attacked me. They were at least two feet long, had yellow eyes and sharp teeth, and were horrific. They ran next to my bike, jumped up, and snapped at my calves; they were in front of me, behind me, everywhere. I biked as fast as I could, but I couldn't get away. In the confusion I forgot where the brakes were, I forgot to steer, I drove right into a ditch, I got back up, and, completely confused and terrified, I continued to the hospital where I manically gasped about "rats, rats, rats, they are coming for me!" Even a compete novice could use psychology textbooks to diagnose my condition as a fit with hallucinations and delusions and a lack of contact with reality. But if you go a little further, the reality was that I just, with a lot of fear and many misgivings, had once more joined the rat race. I had been part of it once before, this hopeless battle to succeed, to be good for the sake of goodness, and to receive good grades without necessarily becoming wise. I hated it back then, and I hated it now, without being able to see it clearly or express it in words. But I still had knowledge of all of these things I lacked words to explain. It is a given that if you jump into the rat race—which was what I did that night—you will be forced to race against disgusting, scary rats on the way home, and that's not a lack of touch with reality at all—even though it is out of touch with the words. And that's not the same thing. Once I had a minute to think about this, and received help to work on it, I saw the correlation clearly, and it wasn't complicated at all. But it does demand that you take the experience seriously, as a real and important experience, and don't dismiss it as an unwanted symptom to be removed with drugs.

I still heard voices as well. Sometimes there was a roaring, screaming chaos inside my head, like an iPod with the volume way too loud that I couldn't remove no matter how hard I tried. Sometimes, I tried banging my head against the wall to make the hollow bumping sound lower the chaos somewhat. It helped now and then, but not always. Other times I would try to pull my hair or scratch holes in my head. That never helped at all, but I guess it was a sort of desperate attempt to make holes that would release some of the pressure I was experiencing before it all exploded. That was how it felt.

At other times it would be a weak, creepy mumbling, or a clear voice with clear messages. "You are going to die," it might say. Or: "Cut your arms and draw a ring around yourself with the blood. If you don't, your family will die." That was a tricky one. What would you do if you received such a message? At that time, I was used to scratching and cutting myself; that was nothing. It hurt of course, but I survived. I knew that I could do it. I didn't know if the voice was speaking the truth, but I wasn't willing to take the chance. So I did as it told me. And it worked—my family was still alive the next day. That was even worse. It had worked, even though I had no proof that they would have died if I hadn't obeyed. I could only see the proof if I actually refused, but if not cutting had an effect, it would be a risky experiment that could kill my entire family. I was never willing to take that risk, so I continued to obey the voice. And for each time it worked, it became harder to not do it the next time. I was afraid to admit that I may have been cutting myself for so long for no real reason. That would be too sad and too hurtful. So I just continued and didn't think about it further.

In hindsight I have thought, "Why did the voices say these things? Why did I have to hurt myself for my family to live?" I am sure there are many answers to these questions, and some are most likely related to low self-esteem and the feeling of being stupid and unworthy. But, more importantly, I think it gave me the opportunity to take action, to do something important for the people I loved. During this time I was in a closed ward, and I had gone from being a person that *did* a lot to becoming a patient that mostly received from others. Before this, I had been in school, had a job, had hobbies, and helped around the house; now I was sitting in a closed ward and was a thing that the state was paying to care for. My family was there for me, as much as they could, with letters and visits and phone calls, but I couldn't do anything for them in return. Of course, it didn't give them joy that I was hurting myself—they would have appreciated me stopping the self-injuring—but the delusions that I could actively do something for the ones I loved gave my life, as messed up as it was, a continued meaning. And it gave me control over an uncontrollable everyday, over a life that was abruptly turned upside down. I still had something to give by following the voices. And I still had a way of controlling my own reality. Obviously, I didn't understand this while it was going on; if I had realized or admitted that it was a delusion, my whole purpose as a lifesaver for my family would have disappeared. This understanding came much later, and when it came, it was the right time and it felt good.

It helped me reinterpret parts of my story in a way that made it easier to relate to it, that gave me less anxiety and self-contempt. Because it was, after all, better to think that some of the self-injury was a confused and sick attempt to take control over an uncontrollable situation and an attempt to do something for the ones I loved, than "I did it because I am schizophrenic." That doesn't help much for one's self-esteem.

The Captain continued to set demands for me and gave orders about how much I should work and how little I should sleep and eat. The rules became more and more strict, and he had new demands depending on the situation. In the beginning it was mostly related to sleeping, eating, and studying. He pointed out all of the mistakes I was making and continued to demand less sleep and less food. He was there all the time. He shouted in my head, and it was impossible to escape him, and it was impossible to get enough distance from him to think about how unreasonable he was, how unreasonable his demands were. So, I just did as I was told, too tired and confused to think clearly. Later, I have come to understand that these symptoms were self-reinforcing. With so much work and so little rest and sleep, I increased the risk for developing hallucinations, and the ability to relate to them in a better and more constructive manner decreased. But, of course, I didn't realize that at the time. I was a tired and confused teenager who desperately wanted the Captain to stop shouting, and I forced myself forward. School, homework, chores, job, and more homework—it was an endless string of demands from four in the morning till past midnight; more, more, more. Sometimes I was so tired that it felt like I was going to collapse. During one gym class, I was so exhausted I thought my legs would collapse. I couldn't stop—that was out of the question; what would the Captain say then? But I couldn't bear the thought of running either, so I ran as fast as I could in a desperate attempt to make myself explode so that I would pass out and be allowed to rest—unconscious. But my body was too young and strong and capable of taking care of itself, so it continued running for the remainder of the class, and the rat race continued. And continued.

As the sickness continued to evolve, with breakdowns, admissions to wards, and medications, the Captain also evolved. His demands changed and adapted to the situation, but they when always strict, and food, sleep, and perfectionism, punishment, and reprimands were constant themes. In periods when I was heavily medicated, I could dull down and be more indifferent to his demands; they didn't mean as much to me anymore, and even though he was bothering me, I wasn't as scared. But then there were new periods when the shouting increased and became so impossible to ignore that I had to obey again. And again. He kept on like this for years.

Now I can think clearly and wonder, how in the world did it turn out that way? Why did I go along with it? Why didn't I say no to such unreasonable demands? How could I allow someone to bully me that way? And the answer is as simple as it is brutal: I couldn't stop because *I* was the Captain. It was a private civil war with me as both parties, and the strength I used to fight the Captain was the same strength I used to be the Captain. The demands he set, in all its absurdity, were my own demands, disguised and twisted, but in a disguise that made it even easier to see what they really were. If one dared to look.

When I was little, my mother worked as a nanny. One of the children she babysat was a beautiful and intelligent three-year-old named Erik. Erik was inseparable from a small toy dog called Valpen (Puppy in Norwegian), and Valpen and Erik were together all day and all night. One day his parents told us that they had heard fighting and shouting from Erik's room after he had gone to bed. Then it went quiet for a while before Erik, without the dog, came down to the living room. His parents were puzzled and asked him what was going on, and Erik answered that he had suggested to Valpen that they should go back downstairs to the living room, no matter that it was bedtime. Valpen had answered that they couldn't because they weren't allowed. Valpen was obviously right, his parents responded, but then what happened? "Well," Erik said, "I put Valpen to bed and I sang for him. Now he is sleeping—so now I can come down."

Erik, in the simple and beautiful way only a three-year-old can, had explained the difficult dilemma a person faces every time she has contradicting needs and thoughts that she cannot hold at the same time, and that she, therefore, chooses to split in two.

Schizophrenia means "cleaved mind," and for years many scientists have tried to find out more about what this cleaving and splitting means and why it happens. Many of the theories have been rejected; some have been worked into different forms; and people have split into different camps depending on what they believe and what they find meaningful. Personally, I prefer Erik's much-simplified version. When all of the thoughts, feelings, sensations, and knowledge a person has become too much, it is easier to place some of it onto something else, something outside of oneself. Erik placed the rules he knew so well, but that didn't fit his wishes, onto Valpen, and then he put Valpen to bed. I placed my self-hatred, my strictness, and my unreasonably high demands for myself onto the Captain, and the Captain shouted the words out loud and made it perfectly clear just how unreasonable and strict these rules were. The problem was that the message got lost in the packaging. I couldn't see past the demands, which I would follow with my best and most confused efforts. And this coping mechanism became a disease.

It is so easy, both for the healer and the patient, to think that a diagnosis is the explanation, but it isn't. The Captain fit nicely under the diagnostic criteria in ICD-10 for "paranoid schizophrenia," since one of the criteria specifies "hallucinated voices that threaten the patient or give orders (. . .)." Combined with a line of other observations and assessments, there was sufficient evidence to conclude that this was the diagnosis for me.

But we still did not know who the Captain was, where he came from, or how to get rid of him. Many believe than the answers are ready once the diagnosis is set. "You're a schizophrenic," they said, and then they thought they'd found the answer. But the Captain was still shouting and all of the important questions were still unanswered. Because the important questions in life are: Who am I? Where do I want to go? Who is important to me? Which basic life rules have I chosen to follow, and which of these do I wish to keep? What do I like and dislike? And which dreams to I have for my life? And an ICD-10 diagnosis can never answer these questions. Therefore, the Captain didn't really care much about the diagnosis. He continued to shout until I got help seeing what he represented and help working through my demands and my fears, my life questions, and the answers to these. Once I learned to see where my demands came from and what I was afraid of, and once I had help figuring out what I thought were right and sensible demands for others and myself, the Captain finally calmed down. He was only a marker—a beacon—and when the basic flaw in my life motor was fixed, the light went out all on its own.

Symptoms are, of course, much more than hallucinations— especially if you focus on the positive symptoms. When I was sick, I did an array of odd things that I found odd even back then, but that I still had to do, and that I now, in hindsight, find pretty understandable. For a period of time, I ate a lot of strange things, like socks and wallpaper. And that is quite meaningless—or maybe not. Try to picture a teenager you know. From this picture remove the phone, TV, CD player—and every other sources of music— friends, boyfriend, school, hobbies, and aspirations. What are you left with?

I know what I was left with as a teenager: I was admitted to a strict and poorly functioning closed ward and I had had everything that I cared about taken away from me. I wasn't allowed to call friends. I was allowed one phone call to my mother and one to my sister each week, and only one visit per week. I was not allowed to be in possession of anything I could hurt myself with—which was basically anything—including the light bulb in the ceiling. The hospital staff had informed me of my chronic diagnosis and, at the same time, taken away my aspirations and my dreams. And there I was, locked up with the only thing I had plenty of—emptiness. The emptiness was huge and indescribable, and it ached in my body. In boredom and desperation, I tried to lesson this emptiness I felt inside in a very concrete way—I filled it up. The Captain was still there with his anger, so there was no room to eat food, or anything else that may taste good; therefore, I needed to fill the emptiness with something different. I ate toilet paper, napkins, my foam mattress, my socks, and eventually I started eating the wallpaper. I never believed that wallpaper was healthy, and I *know* that it doesn't taste good, but it filled the emptiness that was consuming me from the inside out. To be clear—I had no idea what I was doing at the time; I never gave the nurses any reasonable explanation for my actions, never said, "I am sorry I am gnawing on the wallpaper on the walls, but I feel so empty and I've lost so much. Maybe together we could find a way to fill my life up a bit?" I was far, far away from making these connections and even further from expressing them. I ate wallpaper. Period. I left the interpretations to the staff and the psychologists. They didn't interpret much from it, either. They knew that I was schizophrenic after all.

Another symptom of schizophrenia is self-injury. Self-injury may be a symptom of many things and is used by many people with various diagnoses—and also by many confused and desperate youth without a diagnosis at all. To me, self-injury meant a lot of different things. One of the most important factors was that it was a way of expressing a pain that was larger than my words. It was a way of showing the world around me that I was hurting, but it was also a way of making the pain concrete, manageable, and tangible. To hurt myself was a way of replacing, or blocking out, the uncontrollable inner pain with an external pain I could control, basically the same way we dig our fingernails into our palms when we are at the dentist. Self-injury also enhanced the demanding message from the Captain ("You have been so lazy or greedy that you deserve to . . .") or, as mentioned before, be something that voices would demand that I did to avoid having the people I cared about get hurt.

At a lecture I recently attended, the psychologist referred to studies that showed that "the majority of people who injure themselves have a preferred method, which they rarely deviate from." Without reading the study myself, or checking the references, I agree that's true and that it reflects a certain experience, both my own and of people I've met. But the lecturer stopped there and didn't really discuss the subject further except that "when the patient has found a preferred method, the trying of other methods stops." And that sounded so cold, and it made me feel so small and stupid, so many years after I cut myself for the last time. Because that was what I was doing; I wasn't "self-injuring," I was cutting myself. And it might very well be that this was a delusional attempt to hide a lack of fantasy and ability to "try new methods," but I am certain that when I cut myself I did so because I *wanted* to cut myself. I tried to burn myself a few times and hit myself, but except from the head banging and hair tugging when the voices were too much, it never worked. I did not need to "self-injure;" I needed to cut myself, because I wanted to see blood. So often I felt—especially in the beginning when I was getting sick—so strangely empty and remote and gray and dead. I was scared that there was oatmeal in my veins and not blood, and that all life and warmth and spark had vanished from my body. So I scratched myself and cut myself to make sure that there was blood in my veins, that I was alive and not a living, oatmeal robot. For blood is life. Vampires drink blood to keep living their half-life, and in the Holy Communion we symbolically drink the blood of Jesus to take part in his suffering, in his death—and in his resurrection. And in all my pain, grayness, and emptiness,

I needed solid proof that I was alive, that I really *lived*, like blood and fire and spirit and dewdrops *lived*—not purely existed. And even though cutting myself didn't really help at all, but rather created more problems, there was a meaning and a desire behind my cutting that was lost in the lecturer's cold assumptions and in his statistical charts of frequency and diagnosis and occurrence. And I sat there during the lecture and thought, "Where is life, the pain of living, and the dream, and where is the longing, despair, death, anxiety, and the burning blood-red stubbornness?" But I guess that would have been too big and complicated and unmanageable for a simple lecture. Statistics are generally much easier and orderly. And it was a good lecture. Absolutely. But I still missed my life.

Some of the symptoms were fully my own—they came from within, from my story and my knots. The Captain was a kind of symptom, self-injury was another, and there were more as well. They were related to particular things that I carried with me and that were important to me over time. Things such as demands, coping, self-esteem, value. Things concerning the struggle between being kind and being alive, and the shiny grayness and the pulsating life. Concerning silence and noise and fear for one's life. These symptoms lasted for a long time, and even if they disappeared for a while, they always came back, either in the same form or in a lightly modified variety. These symptoms did not disappear until I found words to replace images and actions, and until I could continue working with these things that way. It was easier, and a lot more efficient, and it made it possible to untangle the worst knots and prevent them from tangling again in the future. These issues and things are still there—they will most likely follow me for a while—and I continually go back and feel a need to keep working on them in one form or another, but now I do so with words and without wolves and glass shards.

On the other hand, symptoms were often passing, tied to a specific situation or specific surroundings, and disappeared when the external environment changed. I only ate wallpaper and mattresses in one specific ward. At the next institution, the environment was different and the need to "fill the emptiness" was no longer there. So I quit eating wallpaper.

At another institution pterodactyls resided—the large raptors that came from above and threatened to tear me apart and eliminate me. I felt very small in that institution; I didn't feel any support or goodwill from the people who worked there. Every day was a fight against the ones who stood above me and decided things that I could not understand and that felt meaningless and hurtful. Pterodactyls didn't come with me when I finally moved; they were not part of my knots, but just a way of expressing how I experienced that particular institution. But I don't know if anyone realized this relationship or how it worked in my mind.

Other symptoms came in waves. The wolves, for instance, came often in relation to school and rehabilitation, when I was about to be released, or when I was in other ways "thrown to the wolves." They would come at other times as well, in periods with a lot of demands, or when I felt unsafe and uncomfortable, but they weren't there all the time. They were more mine than the pterodactyls were, but not as much as the Captain. They expressed some of my issues and my knots, but not the deep and foundational problems—more the daily challenges that one usually handles with a light headache and passing grumpiness. The wolves were my way of showing that I wasn't feeling good, but they were easy to replace with words. I remember the last time I saw a wolf. It was on the subway on my way to the University of Oslo. I was enrolled in introduction to psychology and was about to go to a lecture and meet with a study group when I discovered a wolf lying on the floor of the car gnawing on my foot. It was not a majestic and fine wolf, but a scabby, meager thing with yellow teeth and bad breath, and it had gnawed much of the meat off my legs so that only the dry bones were left. It hurt, and it looked awful, but I didn't scream, I wasn't scared, and I didn't cry out.

I sat there and watched the disgusting wolf and thought that it was very right. It would be just that awful to be at the university in an introductory class environment where curiosity and real hunger for knowledge was replaced by a desperate fight against everyone, and where the only important thing was to be one of those students who got good enough grades to push through the needle eye and be accepted to an official program. Where the joy of learning was replaced with the pursuit of grades, and where all juice and meat and blood and joy disappeared so that only the dry bones were left. I was aware of this; I had been aware of this for a while, that I didn't like this environment, but I hadn't seen just how repelling it was before. Now, I could see it clearly. Now the wolf was lying right in front of me and was repulsive. It made me think, "Okay, it is disgusting right now, but I have to do what I have to in order to move forward, and to try to do it with as much dignity and joy that the situation allows, and then I will have to try to regain as much as possible my joy of learning once I'm accepted to the official program." Furthermore, I decided to find my art supplies as soon as I got home and find the time to draw some golden dragons as a counter weight. And then I went to the lecture, and I've never seen a wolf again. I can still recognize the "wolf" situations in my life—they come panting into the world, just like springtime—and I still react to them, but now with only words, emotions, and images. It is less colorful, but definitely more practical.

It is important to interpret the content of all symptoms and to find their underlying meaning. But this is also a high-risk sport that may go awry without a few basic ground rules. First and foremost, one has to remember that *the symptom is owned by the person who has it*, and that only *that* person alone holds the answer to what *that* exact behavior means in *that* exact situation. The same symptom may have different functions in different situations, and the same behavior may, of course, mean very different things for different people.

Furthermore, even though the interpretation may be right, the *timing* may not be right. And a chewed-up interpretation will rarely provide much help. To be honest, it wouldn't have helped me much if someone came over to me at the beginning of my sick period and told me that "the Captain is just a distorted version of your own unreasonable demands for yourself." If it had been that easy to receive and accept the truth, then I would have had no need to punish myself through the Captain in the first place. A person needs have time to accept such a truth. Time provided through the opportunity to examine one's life and truths with an interested, supportive, and safe companion. The companion may, of course, have his or her thoughts about the Captain and what he represents, and he or she may use this knowledge as a basis for further questions, but they always need to remember that only one person holds the answer, and that is the person with the symptom.

I have had multiple therapists, all with different methods and approaches. The first I met used the classic I'll-follow-you-where-you-want-to-go method. They were quite passive during sessions and allowed me to take charge and decide the direction we would proceed in. The problem was that I mostly just became lost and wound up in very tiresome and treacherous places. Furthermore, they would leave once the session was over, while I would be stuck in the thicket until the next appointment. I didn't want a therapist who followed me while I was getting lost and who afterward explained the bad result with a serious diagnosis. I wanted a therapist who actively helped me see what I was doing and who could show me alternatives that were more appropriate to cope with my condition.

But this is a very difficult balancing act. One can be too passive and leave too much of the responsibility on a patient who is not ready for it, or one can become too active and push the process forward before the patient is ready. One may damage the relation by withdrawing so much that the patient is unable to grasp who that person is, or by being so active that the patient is frightened. Personally, I am far from finding a good solution to how such dilemmas should be solved, and I am sure I make many mistakes myself as a therapist. But I try to show an interest in the people I meet, to see past their diagnosis and to try to see how their lives are, and how they would want their lives to be through cooperating with them. Because I know that I always wanted someone to see me. And I try, as long as every day allows, to give people time, because I know that *I* needed time.

When I finally received the time and knew much of my story, my demands for myself, where they came from, and which coping methods and solutions were out there, getting rid of the warning signs and the beacon of the Captain was quite easy. It was mostly about breaking my own habits and expectations and relating to my own role and my own responsibilities, and that helped me let the Captain go.

Having the nurses at the youth ward realize that I was eating wallpaper to fill a void in myself wouldn't have helped me much at the time. Most likely, I wouldn't have gotten better even if they had understood what I was as doing and used it as a basis for their treatment of me—for instance, by increasing the content of my days. But my days would have certainly been better. And since I know how it feels to be in that situation—in the dim light without lighting bulbs or hope or aspirations or work—for days and weeks and months, with only a little activity a few hours each week, I would be lying if I said that better days wouldn't be significant. And, in the long run, better days may have been the beginning of a better life.

And then there were the wolves. What were people to do? Should they have said it straight—"You live in wolf hall?" Or should they have agreed with me and said that, yes, there is a wolf here, and picked up a chair and attacked it with me? I don't think so. I believe that direct interpretations should be left to those people who know the person well and have the opportunity to be part of his or her journey for a long while—not just people who are passing by. And while attacking other people's hallucinations might work for some, to me it was, and is, just too silly. A few people actually tried this approach with me a few times, but it was just too silly. And they never aimed right either, since they obviously didn't see what I saw. The wolf was my own, and the fight was my own, and nobody else could fight that war for me.

Emotions, on the other hand, *can* be shared, and emotions are something we all have in common. I appreciated the people who tried to share their emotions with me; "I can't see the wolves, but if I had been able to, I would have been terrified. Are you terrified?" Fear, helplessness, powerlessness, sorrow, despair, and shame—these are emotions we all understand, and here we can meet. When we understand emotions, we go past the diagnosis and the symptoms and the categories and start being human. And humans, and human emotions, are recognizable to most people and may be shared easily. When I saw wolves, I felt small and helpless and scared and lonely. When I am small and helpless and scared and lonely, I want someone to see how I am feeling, to be with me, to show an interest, and, if possible, to give security and care. The wolves weren't really any more complicated than that. They were just emotions—recognizable human feelings. That was all.

Deprived language, distressed language

The boy in the room next to me was very bothered by aliens. They would come all hours of the day and in different shapes and forms, but they also came when he was cleaning up his room. That's not strange. Teenage boys are generally not very excited about cleaning their rooms and will often use any means necessary to get out of the chore. They may suddenly remember that they have homework, or that they promised a friend to do something important, or that they need to go to practice, walk the dog, or just see that one TV show—or they just disappear out the door without "hearing" what they were asked to do. Completely normal. But my neighbor had none of these options. He didn't have homework, practice, friends, or a dog; the TV was locked in a room and the entrance door was locked as well. However, he did have one thing that very few teenagers have: he had aliens, and he had a diagnosis that made attacks from aliens a valid reason to not clean his room. I am absolutely not implying that he didn't see, or experience, his aliens, because I definitely believe that he did. Neither am I saying that the aliens existed first and foremost to allow him to skip chores he didn't like. I lived right next to him and my perception was that he was very troubled and that he was scared of the attackers from outer space. But it also became possible for me to hear the difference between the attacks controlled by his story and inner conflict and the attacks I interpreted as very relevant attempts to use the one opportunity he had to get away from doing things. And it worked—he would usually get away—the same way I would if there were many wolves in the hallway when it was my turn to clean. Or that is to say, we didn't get away from doing chores completely; they were merely postponed until a better time, which would have never happened if we had simply asked for an extension—both he and I knew that much.

In some ways we were both deprived of our own language, and we had replaced it with something different. And "something different" was often shown in our symptoms.

One way to understand the symptoms of mentally ill patients may be to view them as reactions to any given life situation the person is in at a particular moment; their symptoms may be connected to what that person has learned is an effective or not effective way to deal with a given situation. In this way, the symptoms become a kind of language as well, but in this context they become a language that is there to express a need or want that the person has, and the symptom is then a way of satisfying this need.

Most admitted patients are deprived of their typical language, and they replace it with a kind of mock language that is adapted to the social codes of the institution, a language that works better because that is how the employees around you expect you to communicate. It can be very simple, like how "scared" might be called "anxiety," and that "hurt" or "sad" will often be "anxiety" as well. Or that the voices "make so much noise." These changes in language are quite harmless. The danger is that the patients will get their way through their symptoms, and then the language loses its effect. We were lured into a game where "don't want to" is pronounced "wolf" or "alien" and where "I want to" was translated to "I have to, because of the sickness."

There were set rules at the ward for when we could take a shower. We had set days and times when we could use the bathtub and the shower, and any bathing outside of these times we would have to do in the sink in our rooms. But sometimes, just like now, I would want a shower outside of the normal times. They would not allow me this if I said, "I want a shower. Is that okay?" In those cases, I would always be referred to rules and regulations and appointments and times. But if I cried, maybe even scratched myself a little, and said that the voices were nagging me and I felt dirty, unworthy, and disgusting, this may increase my chance of being able to shower outside of the normal time. But I would always be left with a feeling that I had done something wrong, shameful, and disgusting. I had lied a little, had deceived them, and it didn't feel good, and I really couldn't stand by it, because it didn't fit the image I had of myself. I was more comfortable when I kept my cards open. But this instance didn't really allow an open game, and so I ended up feeling like a bad person because I wanted to take a bath at the wrong time, which was honestly not necessary or therapeutically beneficial. Another issue with this situation is that it indirectly sends the message that there is something wrong with "wanting" or "not wanting." And there isn't. It is very common and completely normal to either want or not want something. We want to do some things more than we wish to do other things. Of course, we sometimes have to do things we don't want to, or we can't do what we want, but that doesn't mean that we are not allowed to want it. It is important to feel our wants, because it is a good way of recognizing how we can give our lives meaning and happiness. Still, I meet people every day who have purged "want" and "desire" from their vocabulary and have replace them with "have to, because of the sickness." And I find that very saddening.

At a completely separate ward for adults, the nurse that led the morning meetings would ask all of us if we wanted to attend the morning workout after the meeting. The question was completely unnecessary, because the workout was mandatory and everyone had to participate, with the exception of one guy with a bad leg— a very bad leg. (His leg was so bad, in fact, that it was impossible for him to be a part of even the easiest workout, despite the fact that he had just been out for a cigarette and the whole morning he had walked around the ward, in a regular, active pace.) The nurse would always ask multiple questions, questions that in reality were quite silly, since we all understood what was going on, until she broke the basic rule; she decided to use the deprived language and plainly asked what we were all thinking. "I don't think you *want* to work out," she said to the man. "Can't you just say that you *don't want to*?" And the man, who regained his language when she used hers, said that no, he couldn't do that, because she would never accept that as a valid reason not to exercise. "Oh yes," was her answer. "Just say it, use your words." And he did say it, and so did the rest of us. And that morning, only the employees participated in the morning workout.

The next morning everything was back to normal, and that was fine with me, because I liked the morning workouts. I hadn't refused that day because I didn't like it. I had refused because it felt so good to be able to express plainly what I wanted and what I didn't want, and to be certain that it would be respected. I refused because it felt so good that the words had regained their meaning and could be used freely, for that moment at least. And I refused because it had been so long since I had the opportunity, and I had no idea how long it would be until such an opportunity would present itself again.

Some of the reason why "want" disappears for some people most likely occurs due to the way people are greeted by others in the treatment system and in the rest of the world, but some of it also stems from personal anxiety about forbidden and shameful needs, a fear that is often enhanced by confrontations with people who are there to treat a person's anxiety. And now we are talking about the fully deprived language, the language that is far from simple and often not even conscious, but that is still there, like a shameful distortion of all the things we can never admit— for instance, that one is *lonely and wants to be seen.*

I quickly learned that if I was scared, sad, and lonely and told the nurses that I was struggling, they would ask me to focus my mind on something else; sit in the living room for a while, play cards, or read a little, is what they'd tell me. That was far from what I needed, and it didn't help me with the scary, lonely chaos of voices and confusion, and I am sure they were aware of that. But that was the advice they had the time to give me, because psychiatry had then, just like now, very few resources and many patients, and the nurses just did not have the time to take care of everyone who was having a rough time or feeling sad. Maybe they also thought that I should gain some independence and learn not to contact them every time life was hard, but rather to develop my own coping methods. If this was their reasoning, then it was very reasonable, and looking back I agree that was just what I needed. But I didn't have any coping methods at that time, and I didn't understand my own chaos, so I needed help and counseling. I couldn't possibly figure this out on my own. Nobody would place a complete beginner in a car alone, close the door, and say, "Have a nice drive and teach yourself to drive carefully and responsibly." That would be completely meaningless and reckless. And it was just as meaningless and reckless to hope that I, on my own, would find good strategies for coping with life, chaos, and reality. And I didn't. So, when the loneliness grew bigger and the voices were roaring and I really needed someone to talk to, I would cut myself. The nurses couldn't ignore me then—at least not completely. They would have to clean up the glass shards and attend to my wounds, and they would often sit with me for a while after. Some of them would realize that I meant what I was saying when the blood was gushing from my wounds, that I was really hurting and that I really needed someone. And often, very often, cutting myself worked. It didn't work every time, of course, but at least it was a lot more effective than talking, because that never worked at all. My words were generally not worth much at that time, and so all I had left were my actions. In a medical journal this is called acting out and manipulating. In my reality I had learned that actions were the only way to be understood. I have to admit, I am very tired of that word, "manipulating," and I wish that it would be replaced by another common and more positive word, namely "user involvement." Because really it is all about the same thing, namely the person's wish to influence and control one's own life and to have a real impact on one's own life and treatment. And a person will use the means put at one's disposal in order to try to attain that control.

In psychology there is a term that is referred to as "the fundamental attribution mistake." This sounds incredibly complicated, but in reality it is quite simple. It is a description of a very common mistake we humans often make when we are evaluating the reasons behind human actions. We often assume that the reasons behind our own faulty or unwanted actions are a result of the external situation we are in. If we are late, it is because of bad traffic; if we forget about a promise, it is because we have too many tasks. And we can think this and say this, because we know how bad the traffic is, or how busy we are, and also because we often carry a very honest and healthy wish to maintain our self-respect and find excuses for our less fortunate actions. On the other hand, if others do anything stupid, we don't know all of the details of the situation and we do not carry the responsibility for their self-respect, so we use personality generalizations to describe their actions, such as "he's a slacker, she's not trustworthy," and so on. This is especially evident if for some reason we feel that this person is "not like us," and since the "them and us" issue is quite prevalent within the psychological health institution, you will naturally be vulnerable to this error of explanation. And so it is natural to call someone "manipulative" instead of seeing if that person has any other opportunities to influence the situation he is in, and if it was really even fitting with his personality and not a situational description instead. But even if the fundamental attribution mistake is just that—fundamental, basic, and common—it is still wrong.

Behavioral therapy has shown us that actions receiving a response perceived as positive for the person performing the action will most likely be repeated, while actions that receive little response, or unwanted response, will often disappear on their own and be replaced with more beneficial behavior. Through the years, multiple experiments with rats, dogs, children, employees, patients, pyschology students, and various other groups have confirmed the same thing, which is really quite logical: If we want something, we will most likely repeat behavior that has proven effective in obtaining it rather than behavior that, through experience, has not helped obtain what we want. Our experiences show us which actions are smart, which work, and which don't. Therefore, it was little use for the nurses to tell me that it wasn't smart to hurt myself, that it was stupid and ineffective, when all my experience showed me that this behavior was exactly what was needed for me to get what I wanted. I never said this out loud, of course. I always agreed with the nurses—it is stupid to self-injure or to listen to the voices or to run, or whatever I had done in each situation. And I could talk about this and be very sensible, but it was usually *just* words. I didn't stop doing what I was doing. Because it worked. But I never told anyone that. I could barely admit it to myself because it meant that I would have to admit two things: both what I wanted and what I wished to achieve, and that I had some sort of control over my situation. And that was too shameful and too embarrassing. I would rather blame the disease and voices and basically anything else, as long as I didn't have to admit the ugly and vile needs I had: the need for attention and care, the need to be seen, the need to escape the loneliness. I didn't want to admit that "she just does it to get attention." Not even to myself.

In contrast to the mock language, which was more or less conscious, I kept this depressed language far from my consciousness as best I could. That the wolves often arrived when I was supposed to clean was difficult. Even though I could—sometimes, and without saying it out loud—see a pattern of when the wolves came, I couldn't or wouldn't see that there was any way I could prevent their arrival. My experience was, and had to be, that the wolves were far from my control. I needed to see them as real wolves, and I couldn't admit to myself that I had any influence over their existence. That would mean that I would also have to admit to myself that I was lazy, and then I had to admit that I was crazy, and that would be too much to ask. But when it came to my wish to be seen, to be cared for, to gain attention, to insist that I was worth someone's time, it was strong enough to make me consciously behave in a way that forced the reaction I wanted; this was a concept that was so terrible and forbidden that my consciousness wouldn't allow me to even consider it. I kept this feeling far away, shut behind with double doors and all the locks my soul could produce. But despite this, I couldn't help but feel a sharp stab of anxiety-filled shame when the nurses would say that I did it "on purpose" or to get attention. It hurt because all my locking mechanisms couldn't help conceal my fear that they might be right. That my actions were conscious. And I couldn't deal with such a fact because it was only half the truth, kind of like standing in front of a raging bear without knowing that, in reality, the bear was completely tame and that his trainer was standing right behind you. And what could have tamed the anxiety a little bit in this situation would have been the other half of the truth, namely that my wishes were completely normal and that I, when given the opportunity, would be able to satisfy those needs in ways that were socially acceptable, just like everyone else. But that truth was behind my back, and it was a long time before I found the help—through therapy—to turn around and look the truth in the eyes. And not until then did I have the ability to open my eyes and fully take in the bear standing in front of me. Because when I had access to the entire picture, the scary part, my control, was no longer as scary to accept. But I needed the entire picture first to understand that.

It is not difficult, after all, to understand that the quiet, good, timid, and bullied girl that was me back then had a hard time admitting her need to be seen and cared for. It is logical and reasonable, and you don't really need any special psychological knowledge to understand this fact. What I find more difficult to understand is that health care, as a system, seems to have opposed these very basic needs. Because it wasn't only me personally that was ashamed; my shame was also nurtured through the statements of the nurses and the medical journals. "Wants attention," they said, and that was both fine and true, but I never felt that any of them made any professional evaluation of this need or determined any way to relate to it in a reasonable fashion. My perception, back then as a patient and now as a psychologist, is that psychological health care generally agrees with the patients. We, as a society, are proud, stouthearted, independent Norwegians who would preferably walk to the North Pole on our own if needed, and we should at least manage without the help of others and absolutely not fall so deep that we wish for attention and care from those around us. At least patients shouldn't. The rest of us who are counted among the healthy for the moment crave attention quite often. Basically every day. If our colleagues at work stop greeting us, talking to us, or sitting with us at lunch, we think it is rude, insolent, or cruel. If our boss stops noticing us and stops following up on our work and tasks, our motivation and desire to work might decline significantly. We want our friends and family to know what we are doing and to be in touch when we are sad or happy, when we need help moving or baby-sitting, or when we just want to talk and be social. We want the ones closest to us to know us well—well enough that they see how we are feeling and what we need. And we want to do the same for the ones closest to us. Humans are pack animals, and we need a social pack. So, where do these patronizing statements come from: "wants attention" and "needy?" What do we mean by that? There's nothing mentally ill about humans seeking contact with other humans. It's quite the opposite. I view social isolation as a much more troubling sign than wanting social interaction. When people withdraw from contact with other people, that is often a sign that something is wrong. When humans want contact with others, that's not wrong; that's healthy.

And this daily need for attention that we all possess is naturally enhanced when we feel threatened or endangered. If a person falls off a pier and is in the water screaming for help, nobody would imagine passing by and stating, "He's just doing it to get attention." Of course he wants attention! His life is in danger, and he is incapable of saving himself; his only hope of surviving lies in his ability to attract attention from other people who can save him. And the people who hear him calling will immediately understand this and do everything in their power to help. This is why it scares me that psychological health care continues to write journals that identifies a patient's cries for help—often quite clearly—as simply "wanting attention" without following up on it with professional analyses of how the patient should be helped or how the health care worker or health care facility should relate to this obvious need for help. It's almost synonymous with writing a journal about a patient who is suffering from malnutrition and then not giving the patient any food, or trying to figure out why malnutrition is a problem in the first place, or attempting to recommend ways for the patient to prevent future malnutrition. This is only somewhat similar to mental health, because a health care provider would never write about or act in such a way with a patient suffering from physical malnutrition. But this dismissal is often given to people suffering from a lack of human care and attention. And I think that much of the difference between the two lies in the fact that the latter is considered shameful in some way.

Even now, as I am sitting here writing this, I can feel how much more comfortable I am jumping in the role of the health care person and talking about how we, as health care practitioners, should accept the patients' needs for attention, rather than talking about my own need for attention when I was a patient. I don't want to talk about my needs, and I can sense that it feels both embarrassing and uncomfortable. And I wonder what people will think of me if I admit to these things. This tells me that the shame in needing attention is strong, that it is not surprising patients feel a need to hold on the fact that it is the *disease* that causes their behavior, and that they are definitely not in control over it. Because it's almost doubly shameful that you want something you shouldn't, and that you might actually act oddly for the sole purpose of obtaining what you want. Like cutting yourself. Or blaming a wolf or the Captain. And this is not just about the need for attention, but also other needs that a person may have. The need to express anger, for instance, or to revolt against an impossible living situation, or to rest. It may also be a forbidden emotion that you are trying to hide, like anger or jealousy. Or it may be an addiction—one wants it, without daring to admit it, and then acts, consciously or not, in a way that has previously been fruitful in order to obtain it. And a diagnosis of illness can become a good way of explaining completely normal needs that one would have trouble embracing.

In 1998 Håvard Bentsen did a study of how dependents behaved toward relatives with psychotic diagnoses and which factors influenced their behavior. He found multiple factors that may have influenced the degree of hostility, resistance, and criticism from the dependents, and one of these factors was the evaluation of the patient as "responsible" or "sick." If the dependents perceive the patient as sick, and their behavior as symptoms, the level of critical and hostile comments declines, but if the behavior is perceived as voluntary or intended, the dependents will most often react with comments that are significantly more critical and aggressive toward the relative. In other words, a "healthy" human being has to be accountable for her actions, whereas a sick person can go further before she experiences any consequences from those around her.

But when the patients have the opportunity to "go further" to obtain what they need, it doesn't really feel good. And they can't feel complete happiness for what they've received. Because they feel that it wasn't them, and they didn't really want it; it was just the disease. Obtaining what you want is not the same as being understood and accepted, and as such, it can never become a lasting or final solution. A need that cannot be admitted to—and that cannot be met, seen, or accepted but rather covered up by an excuse—will always need reaffirmation as it is never fully confirmed. Furthermore, you might obtain some of what you need, but nothing of what you need the most, namely understanding and acceptance. And control over your own life.

The flipside of responsibility is control. What you cannot control, you cannot be responsible for, and what you can control, you also have to take responsibility for. If a person is deprived of or loses his responsibility for a situation, or even worse, his own reactions to the situation, he also loses control over the situation. And losing control of one's life does something to us as human beings. As early as 1979, Janoff-Bulman (ref. Brickman, et al, 1982) did a study that showed the importance of maintaining a sense of control over one's life. He studied women who had been victims of rape and found that many of the victims did not want to be perceived as victims in the beginning, but rather to accept responsibility for what happened to them. They admitted that they had dressed too provokingly, that they had been stupid to walk alone, or other "if only" admissions. However, these feelings of guilt were not rational, and it was important for the people close to the women to make it clear that the women had no reason to feel guilty and that the offender had to take full responsibility for the crime. This, of course, was true, but for the person who experienced the attack, the need to accept certain responsibility for the situation was a way of fulfilling a real need for feeling in control. If the gruesome crime occurred due to a mistake on their part, and a conscious act that they could have changed or avoided at another time, then they still felt as if they could keep certain control over their lives. If this was not the case—if it was really true that there was nothing they could have done to prevent what happened—then they had to admit that they were helpless victims of coincidence, and thus the world becomes a scary and unpredictable place. A place where anything can happen, at any time, and they can't do anything about it. And even though that might be true, or at least partly true, that inevitability might be the best way for helping people move on with their lives. On the contrary, the well-meaning attempts to reduce the unnecessary "guilt" may easily have the wrong effect for a victim. For guilt, responsibility, and control are closely related, and an attempt to remove guilt may undermine a person's sense of control and ultimately make her feel helpless and dependent. And that may then lead to a conflict with the demands for the person to "move on" and to "make the best out of the situation." And, in the worst-case scenario, this feeling of a lack of control may become a real obstacle for the person's rehabilitation process.

The psychologists Glass and Singer studied the importance of *our sense of control over a situation*, even if we don't *really* have control. They asked groups of people to complete the same assignments—a few simple math and language assignments. One of the groups was constantly interrupted by a random, intense, and uncomfortable noise, while the other group was allowed to work in peace. After a short break both groups received new assignments, but now both groups were allowed to work in peace without interruptions. When the results were compared of the second set of assignments, where the groups worked under seemingly equal circumstances, the group that had worked in peace the whole time received much better results than the other group. This signifies that, in fact, they hadn't worked under equal circumstances. The group that had previously been interrupted by unpredictable and uncontrollable discomfort brought that experience with them into the new situation, and they were not confident enough that it wouldn't happen again. This made it difficult for them to fully concentrate on their new assignment.

In the next experiments Glass and Singer went even further. Again, they used two groups of randomly selected people and asked them to solve language problems. This time *both* groups were subjected to noise, just as intense, uncomfortable, and unpredictable as in the last experiment. But this time, one of the groups had a switch on the chairs that would allow them to silence the noise if they wanted. At the same time, they were informed that the researcher preferred that they did not use the switch, and it would be best if they managed to avoid using it. None of them used the switch. But they knew that they *could have*, and when they were asked afterward, they answered that they had felt a sense of control over their situation. Both of the groups were subject to the same amount of noise. Still, the results were very different. The group that thought they could better the situation if they wanted to performed a lot better than the group that was made helpless under unpredictable discomfort. And this was despite the fact that their surroundings were the same and that nobody pressed the button. But just knowing the switch was there was enough to allow the one group to perform better.

Selma Lagerlof describes something similar in her short story "Keiserinnen's Skattekiste" (The Countess's Treasure Chest). In the story she describes a poor fishing village that experiences a bad year and natural disasters. The inhabitants ultimately become apathetic and so ridden with anxiety that they end up doing absolutely nothing. Then the countess arrives. She is so affected by the despair of the people that she says she wants to give them a large treasure that they may keep as insurance. If everything goes wrong, and there is no other solution, the treasure will save them all. The treasure is locked in a chest, and none of the inhabitants knows the exact contents of it, just that it is unimaginably great. There are multiple locks on the chest, and the most desired men in the village each receive one key, so that they all have to agree that the distress is so large that there is no other solution but to open the chest. And with this insurance that nothing can ever go under completely, the people of the village gain the courage to start over. They, like Glass and Singer's group, have received a button that they may press to save them from their situation if it all goes wrong, and that is enough for them to be able to move forward and function in life. The knowledge of safety and control is enough to make them trust their own ambitions, and the village blossoms with new industries. At the end of Selma Lagerlof's tale, the chest is finally opened, many generation later, not because of need, but because it no longer has any significance to the development of the community. It turns out that the treasure is very small and wouldn't have changed much for the community, but as a symbol of safety and an opportunity for control, it was invaluable.

And so we are left with a large dilemma. If we give psychotic patients responsibility for their actions, we risk the responsibility being too much to handle, that they will become the subject of criticism and judgment from themselves and their surroundings, and that they will become fixed with anxiety, shame, and guilt. But if we take the responsibility away from them, and explain that their actions as innocent symptoms of disease, we take away their control of their own life and risk their becoming passive, losing initiative, and falling numb with anxiety. The admitted patients live between these two poles, and the struggle to get better demands a great sense of balance.

Symptoms are a form of language that may sometimes be an answer to deprived language. It is reckless, and very inefficient, to treat a symptom without reflecting upon what the symptom is a symptom *of*. It is important to remember that some symptoms may be connected to the patient's loss of ability to express his needs, and therefore he chooses to use the tools he has available. The other side of the coin is that symptoms are often a very depressed language—they may be about what we need or want (recognition and love) but what we find shameful to need or want. We want praise and attention in some form or another, and we want a sense of communion with other people, at least once in a while. Sometimes we manage well, sometimes we don't. Sometimes we reach our goals and achieve what we set out to do, and sometimes we fail. Thus, it is vital that we continue telling each other, no matter if we are a patient, health practitioner, or dependent, that we are just human. And that humans are sometimes good, and sometimes we make mistakes. That is fine. That is allowed. Even the most beautiful rosebush looks like a thorny bundle of twigs in January. That's the way roses are made. The rose bush may look ready for the trash in winter, but next summer it may be a blossoming beauty. Things change. No one can blossom constantly. And it is important that we help each other to recognize this in ourselves, to create a sense of community that is open enough, and that has enough time, so that no flowers within the community are thrown out before they have had their time to blossom.

What is left

had my so-called good periods. I didn't find them particularly good, really, but they were better than the alternative—to be psychotic and admitted to a closed ward without leave. In the good periods I was still quite heavily medicated, but I could be outside or in an open ward—and I could have leave. Now, I was on one of these leaves, and my former best friend, who I hadn't seen in a year because I had been too sick, visited me. Before I became sick, we used to see each other every day, and we would usually go for long walks around the town and talk about everything and nothing. Now she was back, and we were going for a walk again. And talking. I could sense that I wasn't feeling as good as usual and that my medication affected me somewhat, but I managed to walk without too much trouble. After being admitted for so long, the world with people and cars and birds and bikes and life seemed quite overwhelming. But I had been out on walks before this, and I coped pretty well. But then there was the talking. I had been so looking forward to this. I had missed it so much, and I thought it was amazing to be with a friend again, a personal friend, who wasn't with me because she was paid to be, but because she wanted to be, because we were friends, or at least because we had been friends. But what was I supposed to say? What do you say when you are getting back in touch with a friend after being admitted and when both girls are at the end of their teenage years and don't know how to relate to difficult subjects such as psychological disease and psych wards?

"Look, a bird," I said. "Yes!" she responded. "That's so pretty." But it was just a common bird; we both knew that. "It smells bad," she said as we passed the garbage dump. "Awful!" said I. But the garbage dump smelled the same as it had for the last ten years we had passed it, and we both knew that we usually never commented on it. "Look, they've built something new!" I said. But she mumbled that it wasn't really that new, clearly uncomfortable, and so the distance between us grew even greater. To correct the mishap she started humming: "I can't get that song out of my head, I am so sick of it, a real pain, right?" But I had never heard the song, because radios weren't allowed at the ward, and I hadn't even heard the greatest summer song of that year. And then we were quiet.

We both wanted so badly for it to work. We wanted to talk, we wanted to reconnect, and we wanted to find our way back to each other. She tried, I could tell. And I tried. But there was too much, and too little, to talk about. Of course we had the disease between us, the admitting and all of the hurtful stuff from before I was admitted, and it might be that we could have talked about that at some point, at least some of it. Because we were—or had been—best friends, and we had been able to talk about everything, but now we were far apart and the great topics seemed too violent for a reconnecting conversation. I had experienced a brutal reality I could have never imagined, and I had experienced a world of isolation and belted beds, self-injury, acting-out, and shouting voices. I knew that if anyone had told me about such things before I was sick, I would have been shocked and afraid. And I didn't want to scare her or bother her. I didn't really want to talk about the disease at all; I did that regularly, and now I wanted to use this opportunity to do something fresh. The disease and everything that had happened was too much to talk about, and we couldn't discuss it, at least not yet. We needed a lighter place to start. But we didn't have a common reality anymore. She had school, but she knew that I had quit my education and that my class had passed me by, so that wasn't really a common topic. The hospital routines that were hurtful and nasty, but completely natural to me, were obviously not natural for someone who has never been admitted to a closed ward, and it made it even more clear how different our worlds had become. I hadn't been to the movies, had barely watched TV, hadn't listened to the radio, and heard hardly any music. I hadn't been anywhere—not that I could talk about, at least—and I hadn't done anything we *could* talk about. Of course, she had, and she did tell me some of it, and I listened, but we could easily tell that the conversation was very one-sided. She shared, and I listened. Two completely separate worlds. If I could have only found something we still had in common, something we could share and that could tie us together while we shared it. We tried our best, but without much luck. "Look, another bird!" "There are really a lot of them this year!"

The next time she called my mother and asked if we could go for a walk, my voices were being too troublesome, so it wasn't safe for me to go out. She never called again.

It is not that I didn't want to see her again, because I did. I really did miss having a friend. Someone who knew me and cared for me, because she wanted to be with me, and someone who knew me as Arnhild and not as a diagnosis. I had missed her too, because she was just who she was and couldn't be replaced by anyone else, and because the relationship we once had was ours and had a very special meaning to us. I had longed to hang out with her again. But precisely because of that fact, it was so hard to meet her, to be with her, to still not be as close as we once were. As long as the longing was an external longing, a longing caused by the fact that we were in different places, it was, after all, possible to deal with. When we were together and still couldn't find each other, it was too painful. Everything was like before, and nothing was like before. I mourned something that was there, yet still lost, and it was all too complicated and sad. I was unable to inhabit the grief or relate to all the mess I did not know how to begin to start unraveling, so I kept it separate from my conscious thought and allowed the voices to do their job. It was their fault that I couldn't be with her anymore.

A short while after this incident, I was admitted again. I wasn't allowed to see her or anyone else when I was sick, and so I could miss her again and grieve what was not there, without having to mourn someone who was walking right next to me.

The next time I saw her was many years later. At this point we had both grown older and matured, and I had met a therapist who took an interest in the life I was leading and who gave me room to explore the connections between my symptoms and my life. Furthermore, I had learned more about people and systems, and I had a better understanding of our mutual fear. So I was better prepared for a new meeting. Besides, I had obtained something very important: something to talk about! Since the last wards I had been at had great arts and crafts classes where we did a lot of exciting things, and I knew she liked arts and crafts, we could talk about that. I had been forced on a skiing trip, and since we were both just as bad at skiing, we could joke about that. I had been to the movies, had watched TV, and had listened to music. And maybe the best of all—I had started studying again at the school right by the institution, and so we both had an "education" of sorts to refer to. I had something that resembled a life, and so it was easier to talk to people who lived a life. And after a while it became easier for me to create my own, full life. But I needed some help in the beginning.

"The next time I saw her was many years later." I wrote that with such ease in the previous paragraph. And that is definitely one of the upsides of writing; when you write you can easily jump over many years with very few words, and it can seem like I spent those years in an ice box or something of that nature, safely preserved until the world got better. But I didn't. I did what we all do—lived through the years, one day at a time. I received a lot of treatment, and the rest of the time I was alone, or with my family, and mostly with official employees in health and social care. Even though I missed someone that knew me as a friend and not an employee, the official employees had their upsides. For instance, they usually didn't expect me to have a life. They knew my situation, they had read my journal, and they rarely asked difficult questions that I couldn't answer. But once, one nurse who didn't know me asked me where I lived. I was new at the institution and was sitting in the common room at the time. I gave her my room number. "No," she said, "where do you live, what is your address?" I knew what she was doing; I had been through a sufficient amount of sanity testing that I had made sure I knew which date it was and the address of the hospital I was in. But that wasn't the right answer either. "This is a hospital," she said, "but where do you *live*?" Bewildered, I answered that I lived here, and then finally another nurse helped me out and explained that I had been moved there from another hospital and that I had been moved *there* from a third hospital, the hospital I arrived at when I was acutely admitted. I had a mailing address at my family home, but I hadn't lived there for years. Home is where your toothbrush is, and right now my toothbrush was moved here. And so this was home. Until someone moved me and my toothbrush somewhere else. The other nurse understood this, as did most nurses. In other words, they didn't ask me about where I lived, or where I went to school, or what I liked to do on my spare time or what I wanted to do when I went home. All of these questions would have simply bothered me, because they didn't have an answer. And so they didn't ask them.

But we needed to talk about something, all of the days and nights when they would take me on walks, or be socially available in the common room or my room. There were no birds in the hospital, but they didn't need that, because the nurses were health practitioners, and so we always had a wolf or two. Or my voices, or whatever was bothering me most at the time. Because I was usually bothered by something. There is a third way of understanding symptoms, and that is symptoms as habits, or as compensation for a more meaningful life. Because even when life is excruciatingly boring, which it often is when you have schizophrenia, you still need to live the days. I had to do something, I had to talk about something, and if there was nothing to do or no one to talk with, I had to think of something. And since there was rarely anything to do, talk about, or think about, and I did have my symptoms, I could use them for something. They could give a boring life some content, and they could be something I could talk about when there was little else to say.

I know that some of my voices were of this nature. They were voices that were very close to daydreams and fantasy, they were often enjoyable, and they would blossom when I was bored. I had some control over these voices, and I perceived them as controllable. These were the "nice" voices, the ones I could call on when I needed them and that reminded me of the fantasies I once had when I stood alone in the schoolyard and had no one to speak with. In periods of extreme isolation, there were many of them, and when I was placed on isolation, for two-and-a-half months—ten weeks—they were in excess. At the end of that period, my father arrived as well, who had died twelve to thirteen years earlier, and he told me stories. Because I was so lonely and so fraught, and my brain desperately needed something to do, preferably something good. And so it gave me just that. My father's stories were good.

Other symptoms could be used this way as well. In a very boring ward with a lot of rules and challenges, I used most of my intellectual resources to get ahold of objects I could hurt myself with. I'd smuggle them without the guard noticing and find increasingly strange hiding places that wouldn't be discovered during room inspections. The self-injury was something different and had another purpose, but the hunt, the identifying of objects that could be used to inflict the injury—finding how to take them with me, how to smash things silently, and how and when to hide them—well, that was actually quite entertaining. They say that boredom is the root of all evil, and even though it was definitely not the root, it didn't make things better either.

I could use my symptoms as entertainment and to fill my life with content, and as a conversational topic with the employees and others. Since they were employed health practitioners, I felt like I couldn't talk to them about common things—and I didn't really have much to talk about anyway—and so my symptoms were what I had to work with. That was what I knew, and that was what I felt like they expected me to talk about. Today, I am sure that the employees would have been pleased if I talked with them about "common" things. Back then, though, I imagined that they would be annoyed or just leave if I talked about anything else. And now, on the other end of things, I find that patients tell me that they have trouble talking to a psychiatric nurse, support contact, or employees about things not related to their disease. But they can, and sometimes that is the part that is most important to practice: both managing the regular small talk and finding things to talk about.

Symptoms always make me slightly curious. There are so few set answers and so many possible approaches, and the same symptom can mean so many different things depending on the situation and person. This becomes the basis of the healthy curiosity. And the basis of humility. Because even though it might not always be necessary to understand the cause of a symptom, it is usually important to reflect upon the function of the symptom in order to give good treatment. And as such, it might be better to forget on handbooks and disease descriptions, and rather concentrate on the individual and specific situation. Who are you? And what is your situation? For people are never solely people.

People are people in one system or another. People may change these systems, but the systems may also change the people. And if we are to understand the individual, we have to look at that one person and then the whole picture. Most likely we won't be able to understand everything then either, but maybe we will understand somewhat more than we would if we simply stuck with the diagnosis alone. If we want to *understand*, we have to see the people.

STORIES OF SYSTEMS

Love roses and professional shards

For an entire week there had been a convention at the institution, with professionals from the north of Norway discussing psychosis and treatments. Obviously, the patients were not part of it, but we knew about it, as it was the reason for many changes in the regular schedule so that the professionals would have time to attend as many of the meetings as possible. It was Friday, and we were going to have the regular Friday coffee at the department, and we had been informed that some of the participants of the convention would join us. I had also been informed that I was to be a part of the coffee session in the common room with the others. I usually wasn't allowed, as the coffee was served in regular mugs and I had an unfortunate habit of breaking these and using them to cut myself. I think the employees were just as sick of this as I was, and I know that I often wished I could stop, but I just didn't dare, because of the Captain, the other voices, and my personal world view. So to the degree I was allowed—by the Captain—to eat cake and drink coffee, I would do so in my room on a paper plate or in a paper cup. That was fine by me; it was, after all, a way to mark the end of the week, and if nothing else, I got to eat the paper plate and napkin.

Sometimes they would use paper plates in the common room as well, and I could join the others. That was usually a lot better, first and foremost because I got to be a part of the community. But the community could also be difficult because I was often very scared, and it often got quite chaotic, both inside me and in my surroundings. Sometimes I found it uncomfortable to eat my plate while the others were watching. But you get used to everything, and at the end of the day I was who I was, and we all knew each other's quirks—that was the way life was. And today life was a "Friday coffee in the department day." Fair enough. It might have been quite embarrassing if the Captain forced me to eat my plate in front of the strangers from the convention, but on the other hand, it would be good to see some new faces. I more or less never left this place, so every new face was a nice change. Yes, this would be okay.

I had been sitting in the dining hall playing cards with my guardian, and when I was escorted into the common room I saw that the others had already arrived—the employees, patients, and a few professionals from the convention. I also saw that the table had glasses on it. And I knew what I had to do. I knew that it was hopeless, I knew that I wouldn't be able to get away with it, and that it would only end up as a humiliating mess, but I also knew that the Captain would punish me for days if I didn't try. So, I took my glass and threw it on the floor, tried to grab a shard as quickly as possible and at least get to cut myself a little bit before they caught me. I managed a decent cut before the employees grabbed me, twisted the shards out of my hands, and dragged me down the hall. I tried to get loose and return to the shards. The Captain and the other voices were shouting in my head, furious, and I knew that I was going to have to fight them in my room for a long time, as punishment for screwing up my chance. I dreaded the fight to come and I was ashamed that strangers had seen me that way. They dragged me down the hall crying and flurrying, and while the nurses were stepping on my hair, my sweater slipped up and old scabs were scratched off my wounds on my arms. I knew that this was only the beginning, and that the real fight, with cramps, head banging, shouting, and an anxiety I no longer can describe, was waiting for me in my room when the nurses let me go. My world broke down, and I had only a wooden chair to protect myself against the pack of wolves, the Captain, the pterodactyl, and my enormous self-contempt.

We came down the hall, and we arrived at my room. The nurses opened the door, and I tumbled in, ready to grab something in order to be protected from the overwhelming stream of chaos to come. But the room was almost empty. Chairs and books were cleaned out, and I had nothing to grab. The room was completely stripped. And suddenly an ice-cold thought, clear as glass, struck me; they knew this was coming. This was planned out ever since the table was set with real glass and I was invited to participate. And then the next thought, just as cold: the guests. The guests from the convention—was this in their honor? A small, practical demonstration of Arnhild's predictable reaction to glass drinkware? I was furious. And so were the voices, naturally, since they were me. And we—the voices and I—agreed on one thing: they had already gotten more than enough, and they would not get anything more out of their planned scene. Instead, I reprimanded them, told them what I thought of what they had done, and demanded my furniture back. I didn't get it, though. And I couldn't be bothered to fight for them any longer, not then.

I sat down on my bolted bed, completely calm. I had a guardian with me at all times and would never be left alone, so I just sat there. A nurse sat in the doorway just watching me. It was Friday and afternoon and fall and half-dark in my room without a light bulb. If I had been allowed to be alone, I would have cried. But I wasn't alone. So I just sat there, while my body and heart and pride ached, and I wondered why I was alive at all.

As I'm writing this I think, *this can't be right. It can't possibly have been that planned out. They can't have done this to me just to create a demonstration of my behavior. It was a treatment institution, and professionals just can't be that cruel.* I know how I experienced it, but I also know that I was very confused and may have easily misinterpreted things. The problem is that I still remember the exact circumstances and I can't find another explanation to why my room was stripped other than the fact that they were expecting my outburst during the coffee break. And if they expected it—why then strip my room instead of working to prevent the outburst they knew would come? I don't know, and I may never know. What I do know is that they expected madness, and they got madness. At least for a while, before the madness turned into anger and grief. Because even though I was sick, I wasn't so crazy that I couldn't react correctly when I was exposed to manipulation and betrayal; it hurt. And it also hurt that they could foresee my pain and did absolutely nothing to relieve it, just to make it easier on them. That might have been the largest betrayal of all.

But I don't think it was meant as a betrayal. And no matter what the reason was behind it, of motivation and planning or lack of this, I don't think it was evil. Foolish maybe—a lack of ability to see my pain and a lack of ability to see that what happens often hurts; even though "I started it myself" by breaking the cup, that didn't mean that I really wished it or wanted to happen. It just meant that I had no other option. Maybe they thought that I was sick and that a little more or less wouldn't make a difference, and that I would barely notice, or at least barely care, like other people would. Maybe they thought that I couldn't register pain, physical or psychological, the same way they could, or that the humiliation didn't bother me because I was so used to humiliation. It wouldn't be surprising if this is how they thought, because these were people who were knee-deep in my pain every day at work and who had to deal with my blood, self-injury, and screams for months. If they were to accept me as a human being just like them and accept that I felt pain and humiliation just as well as they could feel it, then their job would have gotten too rough. It was rough already, and maybe that was the real root of what happened: exhaustion. A small group of personnel with many young, untrained people and too little guidance or support. I have no trouble understanding that they, after struggling for so long, had the need to be seen and recognized for the difficult work they were doing. That doesn't make it prettier or more humane or more professional, but it makes it more understandable. More human. But just as painful.

A long while later, in spring, I was allowed to go home for a bit. I was very much looking forward to it, even though it wasn't a proper leave, just a few hours visitation with some of the nurses. My mother had already asked the department if she should be mindful of certain things. They had responded that she needed to clean out knives and pointy objects and breakable things she cared for. And if she wanted to serve me something, she should use paper tableware.

Of course, my mother wanted to serve me something. She's a mother, very much so, and when her little girl has been gone for a year, she obviously would never have me visit without offering food. It was spring, and she bought strawberries. She whipped the cream, the way I liked it, and she baked my favorite chocolate cake. And she discussed the question of paper plates thoroughly with my sister and they were in agreement.

So when I arrived home that day in May, I found my room cleaned and with fresh flowers on the nightstand, even though I was just staying for a couple of hours. I threw myself onto the waterbed and could feel that it was still warm. One year after last being home, and without any hope of overnight leave, my mother still hadn't turned off the heat in the bed. It was standing there, ready for when I would return. And in the living room the coffee table was set. Fresh flowers, embroidered tablecloth—and the rose cups. The family rose cups. The finest and most beautiful cups my mother owned, of thin, thin porcelain with timid, light red roses and a winding gold edge. Each cup a small nostalgic window of timid beauty.

My mother had seen me break cups many times before. She knew how fast I could be and how impossible it was to stop me before the damage was done. And yet, she decided to set the table with her rose cups, showing complete trust in me who had so many times proved unworthy of that trust. And of course I didn't break them. Of course I didn't break her trust. The cups, the coffee table, were shouting her expectations for me: "You are still my girl, Arnhild. You are still the person who appreciates pretty things and who appreciates your family, and traditions, and the important things in life, like beauty. You can never be so crazy that you would break the valuable and beautiful, and you could never be sick enough that you no longer value what beauty is, and you are still our girl. You are not a schizophrenic patient. Here, in our home, you are Arnhild."

I will never forget it. After months and years with expectations of madness, with diagnosis and descriptions, they gave me a few May hours at home where I drank tea and trust from leaf-thin porcelain. And it was amazing and just what I needed there and then.

These are two very different stories about two completely different expectations. The expectation of madness, and the expectation of coping. But the expectations may also be expressed in more indirect ways and can also have great effect. I had been admitted in winter and not had much leave, but this spring Saturday I would have leave for a few hours to visit my home with my mother. It was late April, and the summer had arrived quite suddenly. Over a few days the weather had gone from biting and cold to clear skies and warmth. I was very much looking forward to going outside for a few hours, but at the same time I only had winter clothing at the ward, nothing that was light and suitable for the new weather. For lack of anything else, I put on a blue cotton skirt that looked okay, but not particularly pretty, and an almost new pajama top in white and light-green colors. It didn't look great, but it was acceptable, at least almost. My mother came, and she was escorted to my room by a smiling nurse who told her, "Arnhild has been so looking forward to your arrival, and she has dressed up for her trip home!" My mother didn't comment and neither did I, but the moment the nurse left my mother asked me if I had anything else to wear. I answered truthfully that I didn't have anything else to wear, but that I was hoping that we could go buy some summer clothes for me. And we did. Because we didn't mind that I walked out looking like a scarecrow if I had no other alternative. But it was terribly humiliating to be praised for how I had dressed up so nicely when I knew that I didn't look good at all, because it said so much about the standards the nurse used to measure my accomplishments. I knew how I looked, I was very much aware, and if that was *nice,* then it most certainly wasn't based on a normal set of expectations for nice and not nice.

As people, we are not ignorant to the expectations others set for us. Expectations can indirectly effect our accomplishments and how much we actually achieve. "You happen as you believe," it says in the Bible, and what we expect, of ourselves and others in a given situation, may decide how a situation develops (see for instance Atkinson et al 1996 for reference).

One important element when it comes to expectations is what we expect for our future. What we manage, what may we reasonably expect to achieve. It hurts to work on oneself and one's history, and to look at what one has done and not done and what other people have done. And anyone who has tried to quit smoking or nail-biting or change another habit knows that changing and finding new patterns of reaction is a tiresome job in itself. If the person then does not have a positive image of herself as healthy, working, independent, it will naturally be hard to make a change. Therefore, these treatment strategies are wrong in the sense that they deprive people of the opportunity to see themselves as healthy "tomorrow."

Right now I might be in a sheepbarn, but soon I will run across the savannahs once more because I am carrying the opportunities of a lion within me.

In 1969, the American scientist Scott published a book titled *The Making of Blind Men*. In this book, Scott displays how receiving a diagnosis may become the foundation for an education in being a patient and how this may lead to a reduction of the level of a patient's functioning. He starts with a valid judicial definition of blindness: A person with less than 10 percent vision with the best eye is blind with residual vision; a person with more that 10 percent vision with the best eye is seeing with visual impairment. In reality, it won't matter much if a person has 9 percent or 11 percent vision with his or her best eye, but the line has to be drawn somewhere. And when the difference was registered and diagnosed, Scott discovered the consequences of the seemingly minor difference became a lot greater. The seeing but visually impaired person received help from medical and optical specialists, so that he could use his remaining vision in the right way. He also received some facilitating help in his work-life and home-life, such as added light on the work desk, magnifying glasses, and similar, but except for this he was expected to function just like everyone else. And he did, according to Scott's study. The blind person, on the other hand, was mainly helped with what was assumed to be his main problem, namely the social and psychological consequences of becoming blind. He was offered help from professionals like social workers and psychologists so that he could accept his handicap, and it was counted as the decisive factor in a successful rehabilitation that the person "accepted reality," "showed insight," and "accepted that their old life," the life as a seeing person, "was definitely over." Scott also showed that patients who refused to accept this role would be penalized, for instance through a lack of care from the health staff, negative feedback, and reduced access to resources like work, progression in rehab, and practical help. Most likely, the health practitioners did not wish to punish their patients, and if somebody asked them they would have denied that they were in fact punishing them. Most likely they wanted, as most health professionals do, their patients to accept their new situation, and they probably felt that it would be wrong to let them move further with the program until the necessary insights were in place. Either way, the result of this treatment was that the seemingly small difference of 9 percent and 11 percent vision led to great differences in function. The legally blind also became blind in the practical sense, and Scott ultimately discovered that most of them ended up on welfare, with limited social life, a very small network of friends, and few daily activities. The legally seeing, on the other hand, actually functioned as seeing individuals, with a close to "normal" work and daily life, and with a good social network and daily activities.

Scott studied people with a somatic diagnosis, but there is no reason to believe that this wouldn't also apply to psychiatric patients; rather the contrary. Anyone who's ever been in a psychiatric hospital or day-center knows that expressions like "lack of disease-insight," "learn to accept limitations," and "learn to live with the symptoms" are very common. I heard them often, and I still hear them, even though it is no longer my situation or me that they are describing. I have to admit that when it comes to acknowledging your own limitations, I've said similar things myself. Because there are, of course, people who have unrealistically high expectations for what they want to achieve and who may benefit from support that encourages them to take things slowly. The real issue is the uncritical use of phrases that erase all sense of expectation and that are used to support and develop unrealistically low expectations. And that is an issue because it can create people who obtain less than they potentially could have and less than their diagnosis and disease may have allowed.

I am not saying that it is enough to tell people to "think positively" and everything will be fine. It is not that easy, and I am well aware of that. But I also know that if you are placed in a situation with few opportunities, it can be hard to break free, and it may be hard to receive the help needed to slowly develop further as an individual. The situation or role one takes on will eventually become a well-implemented habit that is hard to break, and furthermore, the expectations of the environment may grow so large that they are hard to resist. These expectations can be more or less indirect: They may be expressed through actions, no matter if it's praising descriptions or emptying rooms, or they may be more direct, through words. A doctor once said to me that I had to come to terms with the fact that I would never be healthy and that I had to learn to live with my symptoms. Big mouthed as I was, I said that I would absolutely not learn to live with my symptoms, that my symptoms were way too painful for me to live with for the rest of my life—after all, I was still in my early twenties. As a response, I was told that with such an attitude I didn't deserve the help given to me. I could never be healthy, and since I insisted upon this goal, I was merely sabotaging the process of learning to live with the symptoms. Everything else was out of reach and just an excuse to avoid working on the things I could work on.

Luckily, I didn't listen to her. If I had, I would have never gotten healthy, and I would never have the life I live today. And that's the entire point. What she said wasn't all that wrong. To be honest and objective, I would admit, after evaluating my situation at the time, that her conclusion was very likely. I had been sick for many years, I had a diagnosis as a schizophrenic, I had used large does of neuroleptics, and, despite many years of therapy, I still couldn't live on my own. She definitely had all of the statistics on her side. It was a lot more likely that I would have to learn to live with my symptoms than that I would ever regain my health, have an active and independent life, and work as a psychiatrist. But individuals are not statistics. And as such, she couldn't be *absolutely* certain that she was right. Even though the truth was brutal enough that the chance of me being right was zero to none, it still meant that there was a chance. And it might as well be me. Scott's study showed that a 2 percent difference in vision could give two completely different lives, dependent on the expectations set for the individuals in question. To me, there was a large difference between having hope of another life—a dream I could hold on to, a goal that gave my life meaning—and having nothing. In that context, statistics and probability become insignificant. I was sick, and I couldn't choose my life situation or my diagnosis. That was set. What could be changed was how this was mediated to me. One could focus on statistics—"It is almost impossible for you to reach your goal." Or, one could focus on the hope—"Humans are unpredictable; there will always be a small chance that this will turn out well if we work hard enough and take our time." Both of these statements are equally true. But they have two completely different effects and completely different meanings. One of them contains hope. The other doesn't. If I could choose, I would always choose the truth that contains hope, simply because it is healthier and hurts less. And because it does not dismiss the possibility of miracles. That is important in itself.

The Saturday of the Orangemartyr

It was one of those meaningless discussions you sometimes get into. There were two of us—she was a nurse and I was a patient—it was Saturday morning, and we were discussing whether or not the orange was a citrus fruit. She said that it wasn't, that only lemons were citrus fruits, and that this was obvious when you looked at the name—citron, citrus fruit. In my opinion citrus fruit were an umbrella term that encompassed multiple fruits: oranges, mandarins, grapefruit, lime—and lemons. I was living at the ward; it was my home now, and from back home I was used to checking facts if we had disagreements. Therefore, I said what I was going to do—a long time under constant shadowing had taught me to always state my intentions clearly—and I went over to the bookshelf where the dictionary was sitting. I still don't know what she was thinking, or why she did it—maybe she was scared, maybe angry, maybe she felt that her authority was threatened. In any case, she pushed the alarm and enforcements came running. I tried to explain that all I wanted was to check the dictionary to see if the orange was a citrus fruit, but I could hear that it didn't sound very believable. She said that I had tried to reach for the light bulb to break it and cut myself, and since I often did such things, it made a lot more sense, I can see that. But it wasn't true. Still, they grabbed me, held me tight, and pulled me along with them. I will be the first to admit that I was angry and desperate, and I fought them as best I could. I was definitely both impossible and uninhibited, but that was then, after my story had been dismissed and I understood where they were taking me. My words no longer worked, and only my actions were left. And there were a lot of action, screams, and fighting and all of that; this is absolutely true. But I did try with words first; that is true as well.

And all my actions worked just as little as the words had. There were many of them and only one of me, and they brought me down to the isolation room and locked the door to the cell. I sat there on my own all day. One mattress, four white walls, one green concrete floor. And me, an orangemartyr, locked up for the right of oranges to be a citrus fruit.

I was in the isolation room often, often with the door closed as well, so it wasn't unusual, and even though it was boring and lonely and painful, it was familiar. The day wouldn't have been that fantastic if I were to allowed to be at the ward instead, so it was fine. I could deal with it. The painful part was sitting there, alone, and knowing that my words had lost their meaning, that I now was a schizophrenic patient first and foremost, and that I could not be trusted. I was crazy, and my voice was no longer valid. Joanne Greenberg describes this beautifully in her novel *I Never Promised You a Rose Garden.* The protagonist Deborah and another patient are packed in "cold sheet packages." Deborah is bound so tightly that she loses blood flow to her legs and she's hurting. The other patient recommends that she call for help, and after a while the pain is bad enough that she starts calling for help, even though it is difficult for her. She calls out for a long time, as loudly as she can, but nobody comes. And the other patient apologizes for the bad advice: "I forgot that when crazy people scream, they're merely crazy people screaming." Or, in other words: Crazy people scream because they're crazy, not because their legs hurt.

It is very lonely, and quite scary, to lose the content of your words, and they, in turn, become a symptom. I still remember the enormous feeling of helplessness and fear when I realized that there was no longer any neutral area, and that I had to expect that no matter what I said it would be misinterpreted because of my diagnosis. And it kept happening and in all kinds of situations.

Before I was sick, I was a good student, and I wanted to be a psychologist. I talked to the guidance counselor at my school and received support for my plans. I had good grades and fine motivation, and it was reasonable to assume that I would do fine at the university. One year after this conversation, I was admitted, but in the middle of all the chaos, I still held on to my dream, as a life buoy that could help me back to shore. This had to pass; I had to tidy up all of the mess in my life and then get back to school. I still wanted to be a psychologist. But now my professional plans were no longer professional plans; they were symptoms of how I identified with my therapist, I was told. I didn't want to become a psychologist because I wished to work as a psychologist, but because I wanted to be my therapist. And it was no longer about careers and education, but about therapeutic influences, or something like that. At least that is what they told me. And it hurt; it hurt unnecessarily, and I think that even though they didn't believe me, this was a pain they didn't have to inflict on me. I had no need for, or use for, the knowledge of their skepticism and lack of faith in me. I needed a good dream to hold on to. Because I *had* been a good student, and plans *had* been realistic, just one year ago, so what was the point in killing my dream and making it into a sickness when it was so much nicer and gave me so much joy as a continued dream? It is not like I had too many joys in my life. They could have let me keep my one solid dream. And my words. Even when it came to oranges and citrus fruits. Because even though it seemed unimportant and banal, I had so little left of the "normal" healthy Arnhild; there was so little of me that was only me and not sickness, that every little crumb gained enormous importance.

Another caretaker, at the same department, had completely different gifts. He wasn't educated as a nurse, but he worked extra shifts because he was unemployed. He also took media and journalism classes, and he taught me ten characteristics of a good news story. "News should be novelty, relevant for the receiver, unexpected. . ."—I have to admit that I no longer remember them all. But I did remember them back then, and I remember that when I was feeling scared, restless, and psychotic, he would bring me back to his reality by saying, "Arnhild, come on, give me the characteristics of a good news story!" And if I didn't answer but continued to communicate with my voices, or scratched, or whatever I was doing, he would continue nagging me. "Stop joking around, Arnhild, I know you remember them! News should be. . ." and so it continued: ". . .News should be novelty. News should be . . ." while I slowly moved closer to our common world through these set, regular, and actually completely uninteresting rules. Of course it didn't work every time, but often it would work. It was something about the simplicity and regularity of the rules, and that it helped to focus on a neutral, concrete, and safe topic that had nothing to do with me personally. These rules were at one point so rehearsed that I never said them wrong, and I was so indifferent to the topic that it posed no threat to me, and so they became a safe and easily reachable reference point to the world. But much of it was about my therapist. I liked him. He was kind to me, he taught me things, he took me seriously, and he was calm and secure. When I started going psychotic, I would always be very, very scared. You become scared when you can't trust your senses or your head or thoughts or feelings—it's quite natural, because when so much of *me* was suddenly out of whack, I had very little left to defend myself with, and so I was extra vulnerable and would easily misunderstand most things. In these situations I never dared to relate to anyone who wasn't predictable or secure, or who I was not completely certain would never hurt me. If I had even the smallest uncertainty, I would choose the psychosis. And since he never let me down, I would come to this man unless I had a very good reason not to, like somebody was going to die if I did, or there would be a forest fire, or something similar.

Some of what made me trust him was that he never used more power than he had to. He would always try to work with me first, and he would try for a lot longer than most others. And he saw me, and he took me seriously. He tried to teach me things and have discussions with me—not only about the news, but also about real news, what was going on in the world, politics, culture—I was given a few breaks when I was allowed to be a human being and not just a patient, and it felt amazing.

One night during the Easter holiday, I refused to take my medications. To be honest, I can no longer remember why I refused. I knew full well that it was a fight I would never win, but most likely it was a way of self-injuring since I hated when they used a shot on me. I thought it was humiliating and hurtful to be held down to the floor while they injected me with the shot, and I always felt like I got more nauseated and had more side effects when they injected the medicine that way. I am sure I imagined the last part, but I really hated the shots, and since I was under strict shadowing during that period, it was hard to cut myself, and so I assume that the medicine refusal was a type of self-punishment. In any case, I refused. And the nurse on duty gave me commands: "You have to take your medications, take the medications! Stop messing around, take them—now!" But I've never liked commands, and she definitely did not say "please," she just said that I had to take them, and that wasn't true, we both knew that. She could call the doctor on duty, receive coercion privileges, and inject me with the medications, but she could not force me to take them, to actually swallow them. This was, at that time, basically the only thing I had control over. And since the situation had evolved the way it had, with screaming and reprimanding and all sorts of chaos, this was a small piece of control I was absolutely not willing to give up. And then there was the self-punishment. Since I wouldn't give in, she started threatening me: "If you don't swallow, I will call the doctor, and you will get a shot!" I was very well aware of this, and as I mentioned, I had likely expected this from the beginning. But beside that I also had a few personal standards left, and one of them was that I would not give in to threats. Because in the middle of everything else I was still a teenager, and I had the overdeveloped moral sense of justice that you mainly find in teenagers, and I had no intention of giving in to threats, absolutely not!

But the nurse with the interest in news was also working that night, and he took me in my room alone, with the door closed, and we chatted for a while to calm me down. After a while he said that it was my decision, but he would very much appreciate if I took the medication. We both knew the alternative, so I would have to take the medications one way or another, that was never an issue. The question was how I would be taking them. He told me that his car had broken down and that he really needed the extra shifts now, and if he were able to convince me to take the pills so that they wouldn't have to bother the doctor during Easter, that would most likely affect his standing with the management and his chance to get more shifts. And suddenly the situation changed completely. It was no longer about me, and it wasn't about giving in to threats and orders; it was about doing a kind person a favor, and I gladly grabbed that opportunity. I mean, when was the last time I had the chance to do something for others? The medication was swallowed calmly, and I remember that he thanked me afterward for helping out. And I still remember how good it felt to leave the altercation with my self-respect intact.

But I have always hoped that there was some truth in what he told me. Because he was kind, and it would have been nice if I could do something useful for him—even though my role at that point was rarely useful, but rather to receive help. Because it is tiresome to be the receiver all the time and to never be able to give something back.

Another very kind nurse worked in another open department, and it was always very enjoyable when she was on her shift. It was a nice department, with kind people working there. But the personnel had developed a bad habit of sitting in the employee room and chatting instead of being with the patients. It was therefore especially nice when that nurse was on duty, because she always found things to do with us in the afternoons that we could all do together. We baked, or made play-dough, or painted. Sometimes she even brought her own tools, colors, and brushes, which we could borrow. It was great, and it would help me forget about all of the sad things for a little while, at least sometimes. But after such a night, after having such a good time, I also felt sad. I went into my room, and I cried, and I wanted to hurt myself. She came into my room, talked to me nicely and was not strict, and she asked me what was wrong and if there was anything she could do for me. At that time I had worked with therapists for a while and I had obtained a nice vocabulary to express my thoughts, so I told her how I felt and that I was mourning: "You are nice to us, and you are very kind. You give us a lot, but you don't give us the opportunity to give back. It is sad to be the person that receives and not gives." She said that she understood and thanked me for sharing that with her, and she said that it gave her a new insight, and that *that* was something I could give her that she could receive. I accepted that, as a comfort, while I knew that even though it might be slightly true, it was mainly a comfort—a comfort she gave me because she was a good and attentive nurse at work, and I was a sad patient that needed cheering up. She was kind, and I think her comforting was sincere; she seemed like a sincere person, but our roles were still set and none of us could change them.

The patient role can be a useful and good one, and it contains some rights that are very important—for instance, the right to treatment and protection against exploitation. For while I remember how bad it felt not to be able to give; I also know that there has been much exploitation of the workforce patients, and we, of course, do not want to go back to a system where people are pressured into working for free against their will in doctors' gardens, or where beautiful arts and crafts from the work sessions would be sold to caretakers for next to nothing. Of course not. But there should be a middle ground between humiliating exploitation and humiliating uselessness—the voluntary opportunity to give, or the facilitation of mastering and developing, for instance.

At one point there was a lot of talk of how there should be opportunities for employment for "work impaired" in my municipality and my local paper. This concerned people who could not simply go out in the private sector and apply for full-time jobs, but who needed facilitation, including people with psychological problems. The problem is money; it's not that the municipality did not want to make this happen, but it wasn't sure if it could afford it. And then the debate went back and forth in the newspaper with suggestions and opinions taking many different angles. And at the open institution, other "work-impaired" and I read these articles. We were upset over a debate that basically concerned whether or not the municipality could afford for us to work. If I were going to work, I wanted to be useful and have real tasks. I would want to contribute to our society, contribute something good, something I could give and not just receive. I didn't want my work to be a burden, and I thought that if the municipality couldn't afford this, that was fine by me. I didn't want my work to cost them money; instead, I wanted someone to perceive me as a useful resource. That is why I wanted to work. Not to demand yet another handout.

I began applying for jobs on my own when I started to get better. I offered to work for free, as an assistant or intern in various places. But nobody wanted me. Not even when they could get me for free. And psychotherapy and environment therapy that says that you're very valuable means very little when the reality is that employers, even in the public sector, are too scared to take a chance to see if you can be useful because you're a psychiatric patient and therefore will most likely be a burden. You and your work capacity are suddenly labeled, and you become your label to the extent that nobody bothers to see who you truly are.

A while after this I actually received an internship with a psychology professor at the University of Oslo. He was a scientist, and I would sit at a small office all alone and punch in the results of his studies. It was easy, and therefore safe, but my office window had a view of the main entrance to the institute. That meant that twice I week, I got to leave the hospital and visit a place that inspired me to keep working for my dream. It was wonderful, useful, and most likely quite pivotal in my decision to keep pursuing my career in psychology. Furthermore, it felt great to be accepted by the professor I worked for. He expressed gratitude for the fact that I wanted to work for him and seemed surprised that I didn't want to be paid. His gratitude and acceptance was very good for my confidence, as were his natural demands and expectations for what I should manage. For two days a week I was a human being, not a psychiatric patient, and that did me a wealth of good.

Psychiatric patient is, by the way, a very peculiar expression. We use it often, but we rarely use the opposite: somatic patient. At least, I've never heard it. And it is definitely never used in past tense: "The man who broke his leg last Easter is a former somatic patient who has had previous bone injuries. Already as a child he broke his arm when he. . ." But the other way around is more common: "The man suspected of killing his wife is a former psychiatric patient who was admitted sixteen years ago . . ." And here you have two truths put up against each other to create a new statement, namely that there is a connection between the former hospitalization and the possible illegal deed, and that all former patients are possible killers or "ticking bombs." And when we're talking about patients within psychological health care and "ticking bombs," that is statistically wrong. Most people with psychological problems are not dangerous at all, and most of the individuals who *are* dangerous are only a danger to themselves. But the label "psychiatric patient" fits everyone, and so we can just pretend that it is a good description of individuals who are likely to commit crimes.

When I was studying psychology, I encountered this again. I was discussing routine personality testing with a fellow student, and I said that people may find them somewhat uncomfortable, as they would arrive at a polyclinic to receive treatment for anxiety or depression and would be exposed to questions about whether or not they liked starting fires or if they heard voices. Clearly, it is sometimes necessary to perform a thorough and wide assessment, but I was critical of making such a comprehensive assessment a general routine. He looked at me and said, "But Arnhild, patients don't think that way." And I experienced, and continue to experience, this as a deeply discriminating statement. For how do patients really think? Do we think, or they think, "I belong, in a completely special way, separate from how everyone else thinks"? If we substitute "patient" in this statement with something different, for instance, say that Sami people don't think that way, or Pakistanis don't think that way, or women don't think that way, it suddenly becomes so clear how insane that statement is. Because we would never say such a thing, with good reason. Such statements are racist and discriminating and endlessly stupid—and this is just as true when they are about patients. Every patient I've ever met within psychological health care has been a human being. And as such they've been just as individual and just as *similar* as all other people. Some of them I liked, and some of them I didn't like. Some were kind, some were grumpy, but all of them were people and neither better nor worse than people in general.

Another fellow student later offered a slightly different variety of stigmatization when I told her about my past. She meant that since I had been though so much, I had become a good and mature human being, someone who had developed into something great through my challenges. It sounded quite tempting in the beginning to agree with her, but obviously just as stupid. Because some people grow when they experience hardships and some fall apart. Some people use hardships to develop their good sides, while others turn bitter and mean. It is not a given that hurt makes you wise; sometimes you just end up hurt. And people who have or have had psychological problems are not worse than others, or necessarily ticking bombs, but it is also not a given that they are *better* than other people either. Usually they—we—are just like everyone else.

The statements above are very direct, very clear, and so they are quite easy to recognize and to distance yourself from. But there are other, more indirect, statements that may seem forgivable in the beginning, but as you chew them for a while they turn out to be just as discriminating, because they indirectly express that patients are a specific group of people completely separate from the rest of society. "User perspective" is a commonly used term. Initially, it looks just fine, and I have often been asked to give speeches or say something from a "user perspective." Sometimes I have used the term, because it sounds quite nice: "Now, we are interested in seeing how this looks from the user perspective, and now we are going to work with the prejudice in psychiatry and hear the stories of the patients." And that is all right, as long as you don't become fooled by thinking that there *is* an actual user perspective. There is perspective, of course—perspectives are about room and distance and from which angle you see an object, for instance a chair or a health care service. If you study a chair from above, it looks different than it does when you lie down on the floor and look at it from that perspective, and I am sure this applies to health care as well. The services look different to a doctor or psychologist than they do to a patient. But that is just part of the truth. The other part is that the word "user" means more than one thing. A user of psychological health care is, by definition, everyone who uses the different services this system offers, for a short or long time. That means that a "user" can be a grown woman who's been struggling with anxiety for years, who is married, who has a house and a family, and who may be on sick leave or welfare and uses the day centers in her municipality. A "user" can also be a young man who struggles with a drug addiction, personality disturbances, and crime, and who receives psychological treatment in jail. Or, the CEO who goes to talks at the polyclinic after meeting the wall, burning out, and becoming depressed, he, too, can be a "user." Or, the guy in shared housing who has had a psych diagnosis for the last thirty-three years and who needs support from the psychiatric team and medical evaluations at the polyclinic. And that all of these people would share the same perspective just because they use a variety of services within the same system is not realistic to me, and it doesn't coincide with the feedback I've been given when I have been out talking with user and dependents organizations. There, I encounter some people who have received ample help and who react to how psychiatry is criticized, and I have also met people who have been terribly trampled and who are angry and upset. Or they are bitter and resigned or whatever fits their personality and their experience. They are all users of one or multiple services in the psychiatric health care sector, but they are different people, with different stories and personalities, and they don't share the same worldview, and they definitely do not have the same perspective. And so "perspective" suddenly becomes a very meaningful word, but "user" is too general and too unclear to really serve any purpose. Because all "user" really means is that you are not the provider, or observatory, or dependent. Or, put differently, you are not one of "us;" you belong to "the other group" in the "they-and-us" division. You are "they." And that makes it not okay. Then it is no longer nice or kind and absolutely not a good tool to break down prejudice—but rather the opposite. It looks seductively good, but really it is just the same as before. It is kind of like using a table-cloth to cover up dirt. It may look better, but it is not cleaner or more hygienic. And so it is almost even more dangerous, because it takes longer before you realize that things are just like before.

The painful part of being an orangemartyr was precisely the fact that my actions and I were not evaluated with a regular measuring tape but were regarded as as symptoms of madness. And so there is no use in augmenting, because the more you protest, the more certain people assume that you are sick. I was sick, absolutely, but all of me wasn't sick. You may not think that "users," "patients," or "schizophrenics" are really concerned with words and categorizing citrus fruits or other things. Most likely they're not, as a group. But we weren't a group sitting in the isolation room that day. Arnhild was sitting there. And Arnhild was concerned with language—those who know me well would not be surprised that I got myself into such an argument. But when my caretakers acted in accordance with what they saw as a suitable and reasonable treatment of a "patient," they took my Saturday away from me. Diagnoses don't cry. But the orangemartyr cried.

Poetry without pajamas

I didn't really want to die, but I had no idea how I could manage living, so I tried to end my own life. I had been sick for a long time, and I was very tired. The therapy was tough and I was beginning to understand more of my own responsibility, but I still couldn't grasp that my needs and wants were reasonable, and so the responsibility became too heavy. I saw more connections, but not what to do with them. I gradually began to let go of some of my perceptions of being sick, but I didn't have anything to replace them with. I no longer wanted a role as the patient, but I had no role as a healthy person either. I had quit taking medications, but my body was still a chaos of hormones and neurotransmitters that were attempting to reorganize after the end of the chemical influence. I had started working, and social security took more money than I was paid while therapy costs took most of an already tight budget. I was broke, tired, and desperate, and I saw no other solution. After my first suicide attempt they released me quite soon after, but I tried again two days later. At that point, I was admitted to the hospital's medical department and was interviewed by a few different psychological professionals. I told them that I wanted to die and that it was legal in Norway. I said that I was not psychotic, that I was completely sane, and that the only thing they could do was to delay me a few days, but since I still wanted to die, that was my choice and a legal action. I did my best to seem cool, sensible, and rational, but my heart was crying and I so desperately wanted them to convince me that there was still hope out there, even though I had lost mine. I was so exhausted that I was left with only the cold, but my hope was that they had enough warmth for me still. Maybe they did, I don't know. Maybe I was so cold and frozen that I didn't notice. Either way, they told me that I was right about the legalities and that they would have me stay at the hospital overnight and after that they would let me go. I didn't see any reason why I should wait, so after dinner I ran from the ward and tried a third time. This time I was stopped by a person passing by who called the police, and I was brought back to the hospital. I was then kept under surveillance in a laundry room at the medical ward while they were trying to figure out what to do with me, and after a lot of back and forth, they decided that they would admit me under force. I think my little but very brave mother, who was raised to respect authorities but was still willing to fight like a lioness when her child was threatened, might have caused this. She walked over to the attending physician, I've been told, straightened her shoulders, looked him straight in the eye, and said that if they released me now they might as well call a funeral agency as well, so she wouldn't have to bother with it. That was about the time he changed his mind. And once he had changed his mind, a whole group of people entered my room— doctor, male nurses, police, and a female nurse as a chaperone. I think they were seven or eight all together; they were grabbing me and holding me down while we moved through the hallways to the psych ward. It was so embarrassing that I closed my eyes, not a very effective physical protection, but it was all I had. All of these people and the bed were going in the elevator and none of them would let go for a second. They all held on to me at all times, but I can't remember if anyone talked to me. And for clarification, I have to say that this dangerous monster that needed eight people, including two cops, to keep in place, was really only me. Back then I weighed about fifty kilograms, I was physically impaired after three suicide attempts over the course of four days, and I was physically and mentally exhausted after a long time of being sick. I was unarmed, barefoot, and wore only a hospital gown. I was angry, and I was desperate, but a dangerous monster? I think that was an exaggeration.

At last we entered the ward and a room. They were still holding on to me and finally the doctor spoke. He said that they would now give me the chance and let go for a moment, and I had to prove that I could lie completely still. If I moved, even an inch, they would grab me again and place me in belts—the belted bed was already ready in the hallway outside of my room. Did I understand? He didn't wait for an answer, but signaled the others and they let go of me. It is uncomfortable to literally be lying down while everybody else is standing. And that wasn't something I wanted right there and then. Furthermore, I'm not, as I mentioned, very fond of commands. Many years' experience with systems that had a very clear authority over me had taught me that they could hold power over my body—I couldn't do anything about that—but that only made it even more important that I got my way. So, the moment they let me go, I sat up and ran to a corner of the room, completely silent, and said, looking at the doctor, "Eight to one is chicken, nobody ever told you that?" He took it well, and he didn't ask the others to take me, but he let me stand there as he answered that yes, he knew that it wasn't ideal, but it was the only way he knew to get me up to the ward. But he had never asked me, and I told him that: "Couldn't you have just asked me beforehand? Told me that there was a room waiting for me and that you wanted to take care of me and protect me? I am tired. I want help even though I don't believe it exists. Why couldn't you have asked, before you grabbed me? I could still talk." And then I recited Andre Bjerke's poem about "The flutist trumpeter who blew so hard that he got sore, but still the tone was stuck. He used ammonia and bleach and scouring and sponges, but the tone did not come out." I remembered almost the entire poem. Also the ending with "you strong man, a wind arrived: a teeny weeny wind came in and softly blew your flute. And then the tone crawled back out and cheered: The wind is my friend, but I am scared of strong men." He let me finish, which did impress me significantly. And then, afterward, he did something that impressed me even more: He apologized for using force instead of talking to me and instead of trying other alternatives first. That was the first and only time a doctor has ever apologized to me, and I thought it was amazing. I found myself in an incredibly humiliating situation and I felt so tiny, but he was large enough to lift me back up a little. I am still grateful for that. And he asked me if there was anything he could do for me, now when things had turned out the way they had. And I understood that this was a real offer, and because he treated me with respect, I wanted to cooperate and ask for something he could realistically provide, nothing hopeless, dangerous, or unreasonable. So I didn't rebel by asking for an exit or to "get well" or something like that. I thought for a while, to give a proper answer to a proper question. I knew this ward, and I knew that it was good. I didn't have to ask the doctor for food—this was a professional place and I would receive food from the nurses. I would be treated well too, and I would be allowed to call home when I had the strength to call, and that would take a while. But I did feel quite disgusting standing there, sweaty with messy hair in the all-too-short light-blue hospital gown. So I looked at the only female nurse in the room and said: "You are a woman, as am I. How would you feel if you were standing here, like me, looking like this?" She didn't respond. She just looked at me with a condescending and slightly disgusted gaze because I was a patient and she was a nurse, and she may not have had the strength to work there if she were to think of me as the same as her. Or maybe she was just tired or not very nice. Or she thought that the doctor was being too kind to me. But I kindly asked the doctor for a bath and pajamas. Like I said, this was a nice ward, with good treatment, but I still knew that they would never let me in the bathroom or in a bathtub right after I had tried to kill myself unless the doctor accepted that responsibility. There were security regulations. They would have never given me pajama pants unless he approved it either, since they have a tie in the waist and long legs and accordingly contain elements one could use for suicide. The doctor was kind when it came to this as well. We made a compromise. I got my bath, but with one staff member sitting in there with me at all times. And I got a clean hospital gown—and pajama pants. But without the tie in the waist, so I just made a knot in the waist instead. And I took my bath, and I enjoyed the warm water, which felt so good after what my body had been through. I was calm and cooperative for the rest of the evening and night, and I didn't need medications to stay calm. For even though I was aware that my life was complete chaos, and even though I was still depressed and unhappy over still being alive after being so close to dying, I could still get it together a little and act nicely. I had been treated with respect. They had listened to me and taken me seriously. They had treated me like human being who could actually carry on a conversation and make her own compromises. I had received an apology from a doctor. This gave me hope that with time it might be possible to get some help to tidy up all the mess I had gotten myself into. The things I had done to myself were lethal, and I had done them with the intention of killing myself. But I didn't want to die when I did it; I just didn't see how I could live. And now, when things had turned out the way they had, I didn't want to die. I still lacked the energy to live in the chaos that was my life, and I still didn't see a solution to my problems, but I could see a little glimmer of hope. The next three or four days would show if further work would trample this small spire or if it would help it blossom, but for that night the spire was enough for me. I had received care, respect, and hope. That was more than enough.

I've been admitted under force multiple times. I have been in isolation rooms and screening institutions. I've been tied down in belted beds. I have been forcefully medicated. I have been picked up by the police after either running away or to be admitted. I know how it feels to lose all control. It can be terrible, humiliating, and hurtful. And it can also feel somewhat safe. In my experience, the division between terrible and okay and a little safe is not in the "what" but in the "how."

In Norway, only the police are allowed to arrest people in public places against their will and take them away. Only the police are allowed to go into people's homes against their will and take them away. And so it is the police who come to get sick people when they need treatment against their will. That is the "what" we need to accept. But the "how" is something completely different. The first police officers I ever had to deal with were very kind. I had visited the hospital where I had previously been admitted for an outpatient meeting. Now I had been living at home for a couple of weeks, but it wasn't really going too well, and during the last couple days the "voices" had taken over much of the control. I was very scared, and I would mostly do as they told me because this was still early in my journey and I was not close to having any idea that the voices were me and that I had any other choice but to obey. I had told my therapist about this, about how scared I was and how the voices bullied me, and in the car on my way home the voices were furious because of the betrayal. Their shouting got louder and louder, and I got more and more desperate until I finally tried to jump out of the side door while the car was moving. I wasn't really trying to hurt myself, not then; I was just unable to think clearly. I saw and heard so much that was not part of my physical reality, and I was so consumed by the other reality and so afraid of their threats that all I wanted to do was to get away from the danger they posed. And so I forgot that jumping out of a moving car is a bad idea. My mother was driving the car, she was alone with me, and she was trying to both drive and keep me still. That was obviously too much, so she stopped the car and started honking the car horn for help. And we got help. Because the car stopped in the middle of Majorstuen, and there were about half-a-million curious eyes there to increase my sense of panic. Or at least that was how it felt.

Most people did just that, they stared. And stared. But a taxi with a few young guys, I actually think they were psych students, stopped. One of them opened the car door and kneeled in front of me on the street while he talked to me. I haven't the faintest idea of how he looked or what he said—most likely I was unable to grasp most of it. But I do remember his voice and his eyes, which were calm and safe, and even though his words had no meaning to me at that time, it was nice to hear his calm voice through the chaos of the screaming voices in my head and the traffic. And it felt good to focus on the calm eyes instead of all the peering eyes around me.

And then the police arrived—two grown, calm men, who seemed secure in their position. They grabbed me quickly and securely and moved me into their car and away from the situation. I can't remember the details, what happened to my mother, the car, and everything else, but I know that we were both taken care of and that there was no hesitation, fumbling, or brutality. They talked to me while they were moving me, explained what they were doing, and most likely saw that I was a terrified, sick teenager who had never imagined that she would ever end up in a police car. It went against everything I had even imagined that I was. I, the good girl in my class, who had never once received a penalty for behaving badly in school, and who had been unable to disturb the class even if I wanted to—was I to be picked up in the middle of Majorstuen and driven off in a police car with handcuffs? It was completely surreal. All the complicated details drowned in the chaos and only the simplest were left. Calm voices are good. Words are complicated, so most of them disappeared, but the voice was left. And a few words. But only the ones that were expressed in such a calm voice that I dared to listen. "Come here." "Not dangerous." "In here." "Calm. Not dangerous." This I could hear and understand. And the hands. Hard hands are dangerous. Fast hands are dangerous. Uncertain, fumbling hands are dangerous. Get away from dangerous hands. Calm, quick hands are good. Calm, confident bodies that know what they are doing and that can get you away from some of this chaos, the outer chaos, without being rough or abrupt. Follow the calm hands, they will help you. Everything else, all the complicated things, I could think about later. Now, the world needed to be simple.

They waited until I was inside the police car, away from the staring strangers and people I did know, before they put the handcuffs on me. I have never experienced this as anything other than scary, unpleasant, hurtful, and embarrassing. But they did it quickly and painlessly, when nobody was watching, and the one sitting next to me supported me the whole way so that I wouldn't be rocking back and forth without my hands to keep me balanced. It still didn't feel good. But it was better. They drove me to the emergency room, where I had to wait for quite some time before I saw a doctor, but they talked to me while we waited. And once the doctor had decided that I was crazy enough to be admitted, they drove me to the ward. All the while they were just as calm, and without judgment or moral speeches. They made a terribly humiliating and chaotic situation close to bearable with their professional demeanor. You could tell that they were used to doing these things. They had done this before. They were not angry, scared, or shocked. They remained professional. And that gave me the feeling that it might be possible to relate to this, even for me, after a while.

That was the first time I ever met the police. I have never done anything criminal, and I have nothing on my permanent record, but I have been in contact with the police about eight to ten times, mostly related to admitting me, but also when I've run off. Most of the situations have been dealt with properly.

Sometimes, though, they've not been so good, and a couple of times they've been really bad.

It was solstice, and I had visited my father's grave with flowers. Even though it was solstice and a festive evening, I felt very alone. I lay down on the grave and cried and talked to my voices—they were the only ones there. And then people started arriving who saw that I was sick and who got me transported to the emergency room. I was lonely and scared and was sitting in the waiting room rocking back and forth. Even though I was an adult, I had brought my teddy bear; I had brought it to the cemetery as well because it was a lonely night. I cried, I talked to my voices, I scratched myself, and I can agree that I didn't really fit in with the other children in that waiting room with their flu and ear infections. I understand that my presence bothered them, and I understand that the medical facility called the police. In an ideal world there would be separate emergency rooms for psychiatric patients, but there are not. And so the police were the only solution. They brought me in an examination room, and I talked to a doctor. He said that I should be admitted, and I didn't really mind that. The police looked after me while the doctor went to call the hospital and fill out the necessary paperwork. Most likely I scratched myself; maybe I even tried to break a glass or a cup to hurt myself. Either way, they handcuffed me. I had my arms behind my back, and they twisted them up instead of letting them hang down. I didn't like that. I sat down on the floor and held Teddy close to me with the help of my knees because I couldn't use my hands, and I felt pretty lonely. They laughed at me, said that I was stupid, pitiful, and pathetic, and they asked me to stop acting so childish. These were accusations that had no real bearing. I was sitting on the floor, crying, in handcuffs, and with a teddy bear between my knees, while they were towering over me in uniform. I felt stupid and pitiful, but they didn't need to say that. I knew that already. They said I was too old to have a teddy bear. That was true. They said that they were in charge. That was true as well. They were the police, and I was an irresponsible patient without hands, and they couldn't even dry my tears. They said that they could take my teddy bear away from me. That was obviously true as well, and they proved it by doing so. They pulled the bear away from me and threw it in the garbage. They said that if I was not silent and good they would throw it out of the window and I would never get it back. I cried, and I begged. They laughed. I crawled over the floor and tried to get Teddy out of the garbage bin, something that was not particularly easy since my hands were tied behind my back. I am sure that I looked very silly, because they kept laughing. Twice, when I was close to getting it, they would push me with their boots so that I fell, but I started over. I spilled paper, and they made me clean it up with my mouth. But at last I did it, and they let me keep Teddy after that. I held him firmly behind me, where my hands were.

When the doctor came back in and said that everything was ready, they asked me to get up from the floor. They didn't help me up, but this time they didn't laugh at me, not when the doctor was there. And I didn't say anything. They had a large dog in the car. It was caged in the back of the car, but it barked all the way to the hospital. They didn't fasten my seatbelt, and I was too scared to say anything, even though it was uncomfortable sitting like that, without the seat belt and without my hands. Naturally, they didn't support me, but they didn't make fun of me either. Nobody said anything, only the dog kept making sounds. Through the window I could see multiple solstice fires. It took many years until I felt secure enough to share this episode with anyone. When I share it now, it is not because I believe that this is common behavior from policemen. In my experience it's not. But they are not saints, either.

Forced treatment may also occur within the wards. Again, I think that "how" is more important than "what." I have been threatened with a belted bed many times. "If you don't behave, then . . ." I don't think that is the best approach. Or, after a while, when I had been belted down a couple of times, I knew what it was and I wasn't particularly scared of it. But in the beginning, the first time, I was terrified. They placed the belted bed in my room, next to my regular bed, so that it "was ready," and it was kept there for many days. I was so scared that I was unable to sleep at night, and the constant threat didn't make the "behave, or else. . ." threat any better. Back then it frightened me; now I think it's silly. Because belted beds are a very invasive medical procedure that is sometimes necessary to prevent people from hurting themselves or others. I realize that they can't be completely avoided, but they should not be used as a threat either. A belted bed is not, and should not be, a punishment, but only a measure that should be used if it is found necessary after a professional evaluation. When used correctly, it can actually be quite helpful. Because it is tiresome to hurt yourself, and it is painful to lose control, and it therefore feels safer to be belted down. At least then I know that I can't hurt myself—that action was taken from me. Furthermore, it felt better to be held down with straps instead of humans and there was less chance of pinching or mistakes. The first time they strapped me down I fought it with all my might, but later I calmed down very quickly. I knew that I had no choice, and I knew that I wouldn't get loose, and so the voices calmed down, that is to say, they did if I felt safe. To me, safety was when the nurses covered me with a blanket, so that I didn't feel so exposed. Furthermore, they had to sit so that I could see them at all times; if not I got scared, because I couldn't defend myself against anything at all. If a nice nurse was on duty, and we could chat, now and then, that would be nice, or even better if she said that I was allowed to let them know if I needed anything. Even though I can't remember ever asking for anything, it felt safer to know that I could.

Coercion can also be a better option, even though I'm not convinced that it is completely legal. At this one ward that I was having a very rough time being at, they struggled because I ran away all the time. Even though I rarely did anything wrong, there were certain unfortunate episodes, and I understand that they had to try to prevent these things from happening. They did this by refusing to let me go outside. It was pretty effective, but on the other hand, they never got to see if I was becoming more reliable as time progressed, and I wasn't given the opportunity to develop at all; of course I turned more rebellious and just wanted to escape even more the longer they kept me inside. This was during the time when Ceaucescu was overturned as a leader of Romania, and I read in the papers that his son was complaining that he only received one hour outside every day in the jail. I had never been responsible for genocide, and I would have thought it very nice to have an hour outside; I could have managed with one hour a week even, if I could only feel the sun or rain and see some people again. After a while, the fact that I hadn't been outside became a problem in itself, and when a year had passed, the people at the ward finally realized that it had been too long since I had been in fresh air. And so it was decided that I would receive a voluntary offer of walks—on a leash. I gave the employees my money, and they went to a pet shop and bought a solid dog leash in leather. They fastened this around my waist, in the belt loops of my pants, then looped the leash through the hole where you are supposed to hold and they would hold me tight by grabbing the loop that should go around the dog's neck. And then we would go for walks. As mentioned, it was voluntary. Nobody forced me to go on these walks, not in any way, and I could refuse the walks at any time. But if so, I wouldn't get any fresh air. And it had been *one year* since I had last been outside. It was spring, and it felt so good to feel the sun and wind and to see people and flowers and the world when it had been so long since I'd seen the world. So, I usually accepted every time they offered. We would walk in the area around the ward, but we would also go on longer excursions. We went to Oslo, walked down Karl Johan, and went to the movies. On a leash. Naturally, I didn't like the leash, but I liked to get out. And even though the leash was hardly therapeutic and didn't help my confidence or psychological health, greeting the world did me good.

Not all of the nurses used the leash, either. One of them was a very fit guy—he ran triathlons, exercised all the time—and said confidently that I could run all I wanted, but that I wouldn't out-run him. And I didn't. If we went for a walk and I tried to run, he wouldn't stop me; he would just run next to me, no matter where I ran, and continued talking like nothing had happened. And when I stopped—I was in miserable shape after being inside for so long—he stopped as well. And he never called it "escape attempts." He didn't even mention it. It was fine by him and fine by me.

So, how do you combine force and respect, care and physical power? I think much of it is about listening to the person in question. When I was very sick and definitely couldn't take responsibility for the bigger things, it was usually still possible to cooperate with me on the smaller things. Such as which hospital to admit me to, for instance. Even when I was psychotic and in the middle of the traffic chaos at Majorstuen, I managed to follow short, kind orders: "Stand up." "Follow us to the car." "That's good, it's not dangerous." "Sit in the car." It may seem like a trivial difference, but in that case these kind orders made the difference between walking over to the car or being pulled over to the car. It was the difference between physical power and very little physical power. And it was the basis of building a sensitive trust that made it a lot easier to deal with me once we got to the emergency room. Because I wanted help. And I always wanted to cooperate. That doesn't mean that I always did, because I didn't. Sometimes because I was angry, often because I was scared, and mostly because I didn't understand.

It is difficult to understand the world when you are psychotic. Many of the regular reference points fall apart; the ones you are used to relying upon no longer work, you can't trust your eyes or ears, and the rules have crumbled. Your head, which should be able to help you out of crisis, has become the cause of the crisis, and none of the solutions you once knew work anymore. All of the complicated strategies fall apart and leave only the simple.

A calm voice. Kind eyes. Clear messages. A doctor who has time to listen, who agrees that eight against one is wrong, and who is large enough to offer an apology—that makes the smallest larger. People who ask first, and then use force only *after* they've tried to cooperate. Andre Bjerke was right: You can easily use power, but that doesn't make music. I was willing to cooperate with people who had used force on me, as long as they had done it in a proper way. Because force does something to you. A well-thought-out use of force done with as much care as possible, and where co-operation, information, and respect are in consideration, hurts a little less and maintains a bit of hope and dignity for the person subject to the force. And I know, because I was there, and it was a lot easier to deal with me when I had some hope and self-respect instead of when everything was broken. Janis Joplin sings "Freedom is just another word for nothing left to lose." When they've taken everything from you and you have nothing left to lose—not honor, self-respect, health, occupation, friends, future, or anything else—then you are free, completely free. And incredibly dangerous. Because there is nothing holding you back. Force can be necessary.

I would not been alive today if people were not allowed to use force in my psychological health care. But humiliation and violence is not necessary. People who know what they're doing have laid me on the ground, have attended classes, and know how to do it. It is uncomfortable, but it doesn't hurt. But others have dragged me over doorsteps so that my head banged against the other side, pushed me against concrete floors, pushed their knees into my spine, and pressed my head down into pillows so that the lack of air would make me unable to resist. That hurts. I still have physical pain that keeps me awake at night, and although this is rarer now, the nightmares are still there. My wrists still ache when I'm around police. Being around police is sometimes part of my job, and I do it, without incident, but I can always feel where the cuffs used to sit.

I know that force without respect and care can have great and lasting damage on a person, because I've experienced it, and I am still experiencing the repercussions. And I know that it is possible to be forceful with respect. Because I remember five nurses, two policemen, and one doctor who took the time to hear a poem about the Flutist Trumpeter. It wasn't everything, but then and there it was more than enough.

The horse is an ungulate

I've always been fond of horses, especially as a teenager. I thought of horses, I fantasized about horses, I gave my bike a horse's name and I "rode" it around—and at some point I even took horse-riding lessons. But the dream was to ultimately have a horse of my own— or at least a horse that was almost mine. One day, one of my close friends made a suggestion. She knew of a place where we could keep a horse, and it was close enough to bike to. The only thing was that it was expensive, and that we were maybe a tad bit young, but we could always have it together—if we wanted. If I wanted? This was the most amazing thing that could happen—we both agreed on that. We made an appointment with the stables, and during that week of waiting, all we did was think and dream and talk about horses. The same afternoon that we were supposed to go there, my friend called and said that she had changed her mind, that "horses were actually rather boring." I was completely shocked—what was going on? No matter, we had an appointment, and I was going to try to keep it. It was raining when I biked over to the stables, and as I arrived I met a horse that was standing in a field just as wet as me. Just as angry as well, I found after a while. But first I talked with the owner, who was disappointed that I was only one, and only twelve years old, with only one year of riding experience, and he didn't even attempt to hide the disappointment.

And then I went looking for a saddle and a bridle and other equipment in a cluttered and unknown stable and tried to get some control over a wet and unwilling horse that was nothing like the horses I'd encountered in riding class. When I finally got the horse back onto the field, it just stood there like before, silent and grouchy in the rain, and it refused to move. Two teenage boys were sitting on a fence and cheering me on, but the horse wouldn't move and everything was hopeless.

When I rode my bike back home it was raining even worse. I was angry, disappointed, hurt, humiliated, and sad, and I had a pile of broken dreams that were scratching the inside of my heart. It was the kind of distressed that you can only get as a teenager who's been betrayed by a friend and had a dream shattered and suffered humiliation. And while I was biking in the rain, one sentence kept lingering in my head. It was a sentence from a natural science book from school, the theme "the horse." It said that "the horse is a ungulate that stems from the ancient horse *eohippus* with three toes," and that sentence, in all its insensitive factuality, seemed to me as one of the most stupid things anyone could ever say. It was correct, it was impossible to grasp, and it was completely useless in my situation. Which made it a mockery.

Many years later, when the schizophrenia was over and I had become a student again, I encountered a similar sentence. It was from my textbook on psychology, and my heart recognized it immediately: "Schizophrenia is characterized by impaired social functioning, including difficulties in establishing and maintaining interpersonal relationships, problems with work or to work in other roles, and an inability to take care of themselves, e.g., through poor or lack of personal hygiene." I am sure this may be correct and completely true, and most certainly factual and sensible—but what good is it? Well, it may be used from the outside, as a description and classification, much like "the horse is a ungulate" ("Schizophrenics have impaired social functioning"). And it can be used as an explanation to those who are watching from the outside, pupils and students: "...that stems from the ancient horse eohippus"; "...including difficulties in establishing and maintaining interpersonal relationships." But these sentences don't explain, and have no intention of explaining, the individuals, no matter if they are humans or horses, and the very unique circumstances that made them what they are in a specific situation. These are sentences that present the universal, elevated truths, far from dreams and joy and betrayal and tears. Sentences that are completely true and, thus, pretty useless. They do not give comfort, and in all their correctness they don't even encourage much curiosity. That is the way it is. Horses are ungulates. Schizophrenics have impaired social functioning. And then what is left to ask? A lot, of course, but it doesn't necessarily shine through. And therefore I am always on guard when I hear such sentences. Truth without curiosity may quickly turn scary.

Another truth sentence like those above is this: "Generally, the schizophrenic disorders are characterized by fundamental and characteristic changes in thinking and perception, and by emotions that are inappropriate and blunted." This was in the textbook as well and is so sensible and correct that it is almost a mockery. Even though I understand what it is trying to describe, I wonder: Who decided which emotion is "appropriate" at any given time?

I still remember the large grayness, especially in the beginning before it became completely clear that I was sick, and I remember how the world lost its colors and I was scared that I was dead. I was unsure of whether or not I even existed, really, or if I was just a fantasy or a thought or a person in a book. Because everything was so empty and everything so gray. I guess that may be described as "blunted" emotions. Besides, I know, because I've learned it, that this period with grayness, emptiness, seclusion, and changed sensory experiences is called "prodromal syndrome" in professional terminology, and that it describes the period before the actual breakout of the disease, and that it can last for a while, and that it can often be two or three years before the people around the person inflicted realize that something is going on. Prodromal Syndrome. The grayness. Both are descriptions of the same state, but they are still very different. A clinical description and a description of a life lived. The same yet not the same.

I still remember that one of the doctors died, abruptly and unexpectedly, while I was at the hospital. I didn't know him, but a lot of people in the ward did, and they said that he was kind, and they cried. I laughed, and even though I was extremely and deeply ashamed at the core, I couldn't stop laughing or say how sorry I was for laughing. I am sure that can be described as an "inappropriate emotion."

I know that I saw wolves, I heard voices, and that the houses sometimes became so large and scary that I couldn't keep walking, but rather remained still, for a long time, and was late for work. My words didn't always come out as Norwegian words, but as chaos just as inexplicable as my reality: "Nagano galinga boskito te noriva." And I know that I believed that my thoughts and actions could really affect happenings, happenings far away from me, and that other people could die if I didn't draw a circle of blood around me on the floor and sit inside it without moving until the voices said that it was okay for me to break the circle. I agree that this may be described as "fundamental and characteristic changes in thinking and perception."

And I am not trying to say that it was healthy or natural or desirable to live like that. I was sick, very sick, and confused, and I was hurting. I was scared and sad and angry and distressed. But I was still me. And the thoughts and feelings that I had and that I expressed were still understandable, and they were not a disease. They were me.

The term "schizophrenia" is more than 100 years old, and there's still a lot of uncertainty concerning what this disease really is and what causes it. But even though we may not know the cause of symptoms as thought disruptions, delusions, and hallucinations, we still have to deal with them. And we can do so from a variety of angles: We can think of the symptom as a meaningful language and interpret the connections—for instance wolves and wolf halls. Captains and control, or emptiness and loss. We can also think of symptoms as deprived and distressed language and look at the life of the patient and that patient's possibilities for communicating. Or, we can understand symptoms as an expression of all that is left after everything else is lost, a single great wolf.

In my opinion all of these angles can be useful and right. When I think of my own story, and when I think of the other patients I've met, both my fellow patients and the ones I've met later on as a psychiatrist, I can clearly see that one single symptom from one specific person may be viewed from all three angles depending on the situation the symptom arose in. But the first angle is the prime one, the most important. That is the angle that looks at "the disease"; one's head is chaotic and it is impossible to understand yourself or others the way you should, and you can't express your thoughts so that they are understood, for yourself or others. That is the founding flaw. But when that flaw is there then other things will follow—the disease will give both direct and indirect consequences. Many of the common problem solvers and coping strategies disappears while new symptoms blossom. And in this situation symptoms may be used for other things than what they were initially meant for. If you have a hammer and a screwdriver, you will use the hammer to hammer nails and the screwdriver to screw screws. But if someone takes the hammer away from you, and you still need to hammer a nail, you may try with the handle of the screwdriver. This is the way I experienced some of my symptoms. They first came as an expression of something foundationally wrong in my life, but after a while the original symptoms would also receive alternative uses, and so the same symptoms could be understood in multiple ways. On Monday, my self-injuring may be a metaphorical expression of inner pain or a need to regain a delusional control over a chaotic reality. But on Tuesday, it might have more to do with loneliness and a wish to connect with other people.

At the same time I also know that not all symptoms fit into this description. Some symptoms, especially the ones that affected my thought pattern and understanding, could not be boxed in like that. They were the result of a foundational impairment, which concerned my ability to understand, interpret, and evaluate perceptions, and this impairment contributed to the development of other symptoms. I know that to me, the world was often very literal and that I could interpret metaphorical meanings in literal actions and relate to them. If I, for instance, participated in the morning workout at the hospital, and I knew that I wasn't really motivated to work for change that day, I wouldn't push myself; that is to say, I quite literally wouldn't stretch my hands over my head and push my body upward. To me that would be lying, because I knew that I didn't want to "push" that day, in therapy or in workouts. I therefore would also become annoyed if people expected me to push myself, because I had told them and they should have listened. This was what I was thinking. I obviously couldn't understand that it wasn't possible for others to understand what I meant, or that I had even tried to express something. In the same way, I could misunderstand what other people were trying to say, or their actions and intentions. I remember a nurse at the emergency room who used to make evening rounds and gather all of our clothes that we weren't allowed to keep with us at night. She had just been with the man next door and picked up his clothing, and now she was in my room to get mine. While she was standing there, the alarm, went off, and she let go of everything she was holding and ran out. She left the clothes of the neighboring patient, including his shoes, in my room. He was a man, and he had large shoes with long laces. I was sad and disappointed because I liked this nurse and I thought she liked me too, and moreover I didn't really want to kill myself that night, but still I did what she had "asked." I started loosening the laces to make a rope so I could hang myself. I have to admit that I took my time, not a lot, but a little, because I didn't really want to hurt myself, and I hoped that she would change her mind. Still, I was well underway by the time she came back, and she was very angry. I am sure she was scared as well, but I didn't understand that at the time. At the time I was confused, angry, and disappointed, because she had asked me to do it by leaving the shoes like that, and she had no reason to be angry when I had only done what she had asked me. To me this was a literal action, even a misunderstanding, just as meaningful as a statement, and I could misunderstand statements as well. I interpreted metaphors literally and literal things metaphorically. I had most likely been doing that for while, because when I reread books I used to read as a teen, I see that I misinterpreted a lot and added many layers where there was no reason for them. And so I often misunderstood, and I experienced others misunderstanding me. The world was messy and hard to understand, and because I didn't understand, I was often angry and distressed. I was unable to cooperate with people around me because I couldn't understand what was going on, and they would forget to work with me because they thought I didn't want to. That wasn't true. I wanted to, but I didn't understand.

And in order to really work together, you have to move past the descriptions and diagnosis and into understanding and resources and life situations. For a symptom is just that, a symptom of something—something else—and not a disease in itself. And that may be the most dangerous part of a diagnosis. It so easily becomes circular, so easily hides the most important part. A diagnosis is set as a result of the symptoms a person has: delusions, hallucinations and so on. Arnhild hears voices (as well as many other symptoms), and therefore Arnhild is schizophrenic.

The ring is full and the circle complete. Nothing else is allowed to enter, and you can't get anything more from it; you can't obtain a deeper understanding of anything at all. A description in itself can never give understanding. For understanding, you need deeper knowledge.

My understanding, now, is that my condition, my disease, affected the *form* my thoughts and feelings were expressed in, but not the *content*. If a person with a broken leg wants to walk from the living room to the kitchen to get a drink, the shape of the act will be different from what it was before he broke his leg. He will walk slower and choppier, he will use crutches, and he will have difficulty carrying the glass back into the living room in a normal manner. But the content, the thirst, and the wish to do something to quench the thirst will be the same. This is, of course, not a sufficient image, and obviously you can't really compare a broken leg to such a serious and long-lasting disease as schizophrenia. But my experience was that I was still in there somewhere, and that I longed and wished for the same things I had always wanted and still want: life, development, growth, a good every day for me and the people I care about, understanding, safety, relationships with other people. I just couldn't achieve it. And even though the content was there, the form it came out in was so confused and distorted that neither I nor anyone else understood it. But just because you don't understand something doesn't mean it is not understandable. It just means that you have to work a little harder to grasp the meaning.

What scares me most about all of these "truth sentences" is that they focus so strongly on the shape—the outer and observable and describable—and there is little room left for the content. They become so caught up in the deviant and bizarre that the human and understandable disappears to the degree that you almost forget that it exists. And that frightens me. Because I've been there. And I know that it is possible to understand me, and that I am human, even though it was not easy to understand me back then. And I don't necessarily believe that these outer text-book descriptions of deviant behavior are the best way of creating the curiosity and motivation needed to get pass the categorizing descriptions and to discover the true reality inside of them.

What is schizophrenia? This is a question with many answers, and one of the answers is that schizophrenia is a psychiatric diagnosis. Simply put: We may say that a diagnosis is part of a diagnostic system—that is to say, one unit in a categorical system. The same way a poodle is a kind of dog that is a kind of animal, schizophrenia is a psychotic state that is a kind of psychotic disease. In other words, it is a way of sorting and organizing information around topics. There are all kinds of different organizational systems for diseases. In the United States, it is common to use DSM-IV; in Europe, including Norway, we use a system called ICD-10. This acronym stands for "International Classification of Disorders," and it is, as the name describes, an international system of classifying diseases, developed by a group of professionals with various backgrounds, under the guidance of the World Health Organization. The 10 stand for the tenth edition, which shows that this system is constantly revised and reworked, and that right now we use this version, which is a little bit, but not a lot, different than the previous one, and that will most likely will be slightly changed for the next edition.

This is also important: Diagnosis—and especially psychiatric diagnosis—is very different from poodles and retrievers. Dogs, flowers, fishes, stone, and all sorts of other things in this world are divided into natural categories. In other words, we can all, without a doubt, separate between a dog and a cat. There are foundational and verifiable differences between dogs and cats, and there is no room for doubt or overlapping of animals that are slightly dog and slightly cat.

This is not the case with psychiatric diagnoses. This means, among other things, that there are no inherent or final differences between the various groups, and there may be multiple overlaps, in which the same symptoms occur in very different cases. The different diagnoses can also "slightly overlap" and partly describe the same condition. It will also be necessary to revise the system of categorization at regular intervals. The professionals who take part in these discussions have different backgrounds, and they view things differently. This is necessary in order to ensure that the diagnostic systems are as useful as possible for all different practices, but naturally, it also makes it more difficult to come to any sort of agreement. They have therefore decided that it is not necessary to agree on everything. They *describe* the different psychiatric diseases and agree on the description and where the specific disease should be placed in the categorical system. They also agree on which symptoms need to be there in order to diagnose a specific condition, which symptoms may be there, and if there are any symptoms or factors that are not compatible with this specific condition. Furthermore, they decide on a name for the diagnosis. And that's all. The criteria for the diagnosis manual is "truth sentences" that, per definition, are correct—that we have agreed we will call this schizophrenia, and so this is what is schizophrenia, at least until science has found something new that moves us forward and we revise our definition. They are pure descriptions, and they do not want to be anything more than descriptions. The diagnostic system says, with few exceptions, nothing of the causes of the different conditions. It says nothing about recommended treatment. And initially it says nothing about the prognoses; that is to say, how these patients will cope in one year, five years, or twenty years.

The diagnostic manuals give descriptions of various sets of symptoms, and as such they become handbooks that health care professionals can use when they meet a patient. The symptoms of the patient can be compared to the descriptions and the rules in the manual ("have to show signs of at least three of the following symptoms"; "have to last for at least one month"; "should not be because of a somatic condition") until they find the diagnosis and the name that suits this patient's symptoms best. This diagnostic name may then be used to describe the patient to other professionals and to the welfare system and others who are in contact with the patient. This is both practical and simple. Instead of writing a comprehensive description of each patient's symptoms, you can simply state the diagnosis and then pass on a lot, if not all, necessary information in a quick and efficient way.

Diagnoses are also important for the treatment system. When you need to decide who should have the right to care, it is best to have somewhat strict—and equal—rules to distinguish between sadness and depression. When a new system is implemented, it is often necessary to have a sense of which groups of patients this system should be arranged for. When you wish to make scientific studies or work with statistics, it is also necessary to have a system that ensures we have the same perception of the same term and that these groups of patients who are described actually have something in common.

So far, so good. But diagnoses means categorizing *humans*, and that will always be different from categorizing objects, like coins or stamps. Humans *know what is going on* and they are affected by it for better or for worse.

To some, receiving a psychiatric diagnosis can be experienced as a sentence, as something estranged, and if you didn't feel sick before, you will most definitely feel sick after. Personally, I remember it was hard to understand that all of the strange and scary words and descriptions were about me. This seemed peculiar and so serious—that was how you talked about others, but I wasn't like that!

To receive a diagnosis can also feel good. Finally, whatever is wrong with you is given a name, and you get confirmation that you are sick—not mean or lazy. Other cultures have had different modes of interpreting mental illness. For instance, from a religious understanding, it used to be common to see the psychologically diseased as bewitched or possessed by evil spirits. It is only natural that the description model a society uses will influence the treatment of the people who fall outside of the norms. Disease is, for most of us, an understandable reason to act differently or to not do the best one can—and that is valid no matter if you miss work because of the flu or if you quit school after receiving a psychological diagnosis. If you are sick, it's okay not to manage things; if you are not sick, you are ditching. Furthermore, receiving a diagnosis might provide hope for a treatment of the problem at hand. Because if my issues are caused by a disease, and the doctors knows which disease I have, well, I can hope that they can treat my disease and make me healthy and free of pain.

I received my diagnosis because I met the diagnostic criteria for schizophrenia, that is my symptoms matched the description of schizophrenia that ICD-10 provides. But there are many such criteria, and it is not necessary to meet all to receive a diagnosis, and thus you may end up with varying "treatment blends." This means that people who may have the same schizophrenia diagnosis can have different problems and different symptoms, even though much is very similar. It is also common to distinguish between positive and negative symptoms. Positive symptoms mean that something is added to the personality you had before, for instance delusions or hallucinations, while negative symptoms mean that you've lost some of your personality and, for instance, have become more quiet, introverted, or passive than you used to be. It is important to remember that negative symptoms are also part of the schizophrenia diagnosis and that many patients struggle with these symptoms. When I see how many different symptom images can belong under my diagnosis, and when I think of all the different people I've met with this diagnosis, I am increasingly unsure of whether or not schizophrenia is really *one* disease or if it is an umbrella term for many different conditions that we do not yet know enough about. Research also shows that how a person deals with schizophrenia may vary greatly and that there was no reason for the pessimistic vision of my future that I first received as a teenager. When I was still at the university, part of our curriculum was a book called *Lærebok i psykiatri (Textbook in Psychiatry)* by Dahl, Eitinger, Malt, and Retterstol. In this book, the authors refer to many large European studies that have investigated the development of disease in people with schizophrenia. The results vary greatly between each individual study, but generally they show that about one third are partially or completely healthy, one third manage well even though they are still somewhat bothered by the disease and still need help from professionals, and one third struggle a lot and for a long time.

Can you imagine if someone told me this back when I was first diagnosed instead of saying that "schizophrenia is a chronic disease"! If so, I would have gained hope that I could be part of the "healthy third," and even though I would have had trouble believing it during my most depressed periods, it would have given me more hope and it would have legitimized my stubborn dream that I would make it in the end.

I also had some statistics on my side without knowing it. Because women also have a tendency to do better than men when diagnosed as schizophrenic, and a diagnosis dominated by positive symptoms also enhances your chances of recovery in comparison to patients who are mainly dominated by passiveness and introversion. There were also some statistics that give less reason for optimism, for instance that I was young when I got sick and that my disease had a slow start. But it is hard to say anything about this with certainty. There are so many factors that work together and affect each other differently that it is hard to come to a good conclusion as to what is what and what is most important.

However, it does not mean that it is not important to get to know the person and the individual condition, because it is. It's not only helpful in making precise classifications or prognoses, but also in finding out as much as possible about how we can help this person specifically, in this particular situation. Because we are never treating "one schizophrenic," but a human being with a schizophrenia diagnosis. And that is completely different. A small drawing may explain this difference:

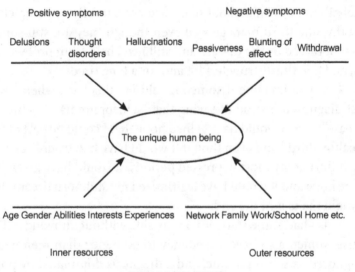

At the top of the drawing, we have the clinical picture, with the different symptoms, both positive and negative. The overview is in no way intended to be a complete list of all the symptoms of schizophrenia; it just provides some examples. Every patient will have his own blend of symptoms; in addition, he will have his own completely unique symptom, for instance connected to what kind of voices he hears or which delusions he has.

At the bottom of the drawing, there's a list of factors that describes the person who receives the diagnosis. This is not an exhaustive list either, but a few examples of important inner and outer resources—or lack of—that a person may have. In the middle of the drawing, the unique human being stands, with his own unique life situation that is a result of the relationship between illness, personality, and outer circumstances. And that is exactly where the person should be, at the center. When I was sick, I felt that my disease got too much of the attention; this also concerned my weaknesses. I experienced a lack of interest in my strengths, in *who* I was *outside* of my disease. Sometimes I almost had the feeling that interests, hobbies, and wants were merely a bother, something that disrupted what I was really was, namely the disease and the treatment of the disease. The main focus on what was not working in fact tainted an already frail self-image, and during rough treatment every day there were definitely needs for breaks with a refill of things I could master, and that made me feel well. However, it is of even more importance that the lack of focus on my personality and my resources made it difficult to find a way for my therapists to work with me. Because I was never, in my own eyes, "a patient with schizophrenia." I was Arnhild. And right then, Arnhild was going through a difficult time.

In order to deal with these difficulties, I used whatever resources I had, and as a knight in an old fairytale, I was equipped with magic weapons to help me in the battle against the monster. I had my stubbornness that would help me hang in there and never give up, I had fantasy and creativity that helped me find a way when all of the roads were shut down, I had a family who was always there to help and support me, and I had multiple interested health practitioners and after a while a good support system in my municipality, with a doctor, welfare offices, and other helpers.

But like in every other fairytale, there was an evil queen who had also given me less fortunate "gifts", first and foremost, my young age. Because I was so young, I had no experience when it came to leading a grown-up life, something that would have been helpful. Furthermore, I had no "adult life stuff" like education, work, or my own place to live, and that would have been nice as well. I had few friends and a small or nonexistent network of people I trusted, and I had a small and light lifeboat to greet the storms with, without the cargo that a few years of living would have given me.

So, what would be the best way to consider this unique person-situation-disease blend? One thing I do know, after visiting multiple clinics and having been part of multiple treatment processes, is that it was usually most effective when the practitioners considered *who I was*—by working with me and using my stubbornness as the resource it actually was instead of fighting me and commanding me. I actually do not think I am that difficult to work with, but I know that I don't like being bossed around—and who does?—and that I can shut down completely when I feel threatened. And now, when I think back on what worked and what didn't work, I think that is one of the biggest differences: The ones who made it work made it work by working with my deficiences and weaknesses, and they always played on my team, not because there was a law that said that they had to, but simply because it was my life, my personality, and my disease, and at the end of the day, only I could do anything about it. I couldn't have done it without help from outside, and no helper in the world could ever have made me healthy without my help. That is what is meant by the word teamwork.

STORIES OF CHANGE

Travel companion

In the story about Askeladden and the good helpers, Asbjornsen and Moe tell the story of the king who says that the one who can build a ship that is just as good on land as it is at sea, and in air as well, will get the princess and half the kingdom. This is obviously a future many imagine, and many try to make real, even the brothers of Askeladden. They go out in the forest to build a ship, but they are not completely convinced, or maybe they want to avoid competitions, because when they meet an older man who asks what they are doing, they say that they are making a trough. And a trough they make. After a while they tire, and want to eat their lunch. Again the older man passes by, and asks them what they have with them on their journey, what resources and provisions. And again the boys hide what they have, either out of modesty or out of miserliness, and they answer that they only have dirt. And dirt their food becomes. And so it is Askeladden's turn. He also meets the older man on the road, but he dares to be honest. He says what he is up to, that he wants to build a ship that is just as good at land, at sea, and in the air as well, since it is necessary in order for him to get what he wants, namely the princess and half the kingdom. And when the older man asks what he brought, he is honest once more and doesn't try to look better or worse than he is, but rather says exactly what he has, and he also offers to share. And so the older man builds the ship for him, and he can sail off to the royal palace in his beautiful vessel. But when he arrives at the king's doorstep, the king is not enthused by the fine ship. The king does not inspect the boat, he doesn't ask for technical specifications or about the top speed or anything at all; no, he doesn't even walk outside to look at it. He looks only at Askeladden. And he doesn't look at him in astonishment because he has managed to make such a wonderful ship; no, he looks at him with contempt, because he is not pretty enough and not strapping enough and not royal. "Askeladden was both black and sooty and the King did not want to give his daughter to such a bum," it is written, and I feel for Askeladden. I, too, tried to be open and honest about my dreams, to verbalize what I wanted for my future, even though the goal was crazy and the chances slim. And I also tried to stand behind what I had and to not make my provisions better or worse than they were. I may not have had a lot to bring to the table, but it was better than nothing—at least it was not only dirt. And as a reward, I, too, received my ship. And even though it wasn't a beautiful ship like Askeladden had, I received stubbornness, willpower, and aspirations, and those too make up a useful vessel that you may travel far with. At least to the royal palace. But it always ends there. You always meet some little king who doesn't want to look at your ship or hear about your travel plans, but who only sees the sooty clothing and diagnoses. "Looking at your medical history. . ."; "with your diagnosis. . ."; "not realistic. . ."; "not possible. . ."; "not wanted. . ."

Luckily, Askeladden had picked up some good helpers along the way. Brave souls who jumped on the strange ship without blinking or asking questions and who accepted Askeladden's idea and plans without silly questions. They all had distinct, individual traits, they all had something to bring to "project airship," and they were all equally important and indispensible in order for

Askeladden to reach his goal. Without them, he would have never gotten past the king and won his princess.

I, too, had my helpers, with their special traits and their contributions. Since this is no fairytale, but a somewhat more complex reality, every single helper did not have one good trait. Some had many, and some had only one or two. Some followed me far, and some just stopped by for a short while. Nobody was a saint, and some of them brought things that weren't necessarily all good, but that's real life. However, they were all important. And without them, I would have never gotten past the royal palace and won my future.

Askeladden's first helper was a guy who was so hungry for meat that he could never eat enough. However, he was not particularly picky, and when he didn't have meat, he ate pebbles and was pleased with that. I have met many of his sisters, and in my experience many of them are ergo therapists and occupational therapists. Ergo therapists are usually very good at focusing on what is instead of what could have been or should have been, and they can enjoy the pebbles if there is no meat. In all the places I've been, the workrooms have been small oases of conquering, in a hospital life that was mostly dominated by what I couldn't master, what I didn't know were my faults. It is tiresome to be psychotic, and after a while I was very tired of everything I didn't know how to do and everything I no longer could do. My everyday consisted of a large heap of broken dreams and broken plans, and the treatment, whether it was amendment therapy or more concrete training, was always based on what I had to change. Therapy is change, and to me change was very necessary because my life was so bad that making changes was a prerequisite for continuing to live. But it was tiresome to change. After a while, I got very tired of analyzing everything I did to see what I could have done differently, what went wrong, and what I should have done instead.

And then they were there, the ergo therapists, and they invited me into the workrooms where the mistakes were easily fixed and the demands were concrete and manageable. That was nice, since I liked to work with challenges in that way. In one place they let me work with ceramics. My everyday at that point consisted of the intense work to jump at the world at top speed, to find an apprenticeship, and to evaluate if I could handle another attempt to live outside of an institution, or if I should apply for a place in shared housing. My therapeutic everyday consisted of the focused and painful work of gaining back the responsibility for my life, seeing that I had options and that I was not a victim of my disease, and mourning what had been and preparing for what would come. And in the workroom the ceramics would sometimes break. They would crack during firing, or pieces would chip off in the fragile phase when it was dried and not yet fired. You can throw out broken ceramics, and then you can start over. Or, you can make something new with the broken pieces. Mistakes can be fixed.

One night before Christmas, I had worked for hours painting this porcelain cup. When I was cleaning the brush, my arm brushed the cup; it fell to the floor, and it broke. I stood there feeling stupid with shards of porcelain in my hands. The next part should have been easy. But I had come further and I asked for help to "take the shards away from me before I cut myself." I said, "I have to think." A little while later I asked to get the broken cup back, and I did. I could glue some of the pieces together; the bottom was really whole, but at the top, a lot was missing. So I made a rim out of clay. When the clay was dry, it was painted and glazed, and the result was pretty good—for many years to come that pencil cup stood on my desk as a reminder that what's been broken can be glued back together, one way or another, and that what is different can also be good.

Even before I met practitioners who believed that change was possible, there was a lot of focus on all the things that didn't work—yes, maybe even more then. I was supposed to learn to live within my own limitations and to understand that I had a chronic disease and that I should give up my dreams and focus on all the things I couldn't do. I am not sure if these small kings ever had the opportunity to try their own advice, but I can tell you that I didn't find it fun at all to focus on my chronic insanity. Luckily, there was a workroom in the ward. I never received such messages there, rather the opposite. There, we focused on fabrics and thread, and if it became too risky to focus on things that demanded scissors, needles, or other dangerous objects, we would focus on colors, paint, glue, paper, and decorating wooden figurines. I made a lot of pretty things, and the ergo therapist brought me back out to the reception area, where I was not allowed, and made a fine small Christmas exhibition of my work for the employees and visitors. She brought the money back inside, and I was in charge of the accounting—this much for materials, the rest for me. It may not have changed my life, but it gave me a few drops of normalcy in a sick everyday. I needed it, and I enjoyed it.

At the hopsital there was also a workroom, at least sometimes, when they could afford an ergo therapist, assisting nurses, and materials. When I was there, it was a break from the madness, a place where the voices held less sway, most likely because it made me feel so good. It never changed my life, and it never made me healthy, but it felt good to be there right then just doing simple things. In the workroom the past was the past and the future was the future, and there was no need to analyze or plan. You could paint. Or crochet. Or glue mosaics. Or anything you liked.

Hospitals are often very white. Yellow-white walls, white coats, white linens. I hate white linen; I never sleep in it if I can avoid it because it reminds me so much of that world. I was gray, the future was black, and with all of the white, it turned into even more gray. But in the workroom there was color. And even though pearls, yarn, paint, and mosaics could never take the grayness away, they helped remind me that colors existed. For a little while, one hour each day, I could forget the chaos and just *be*. In a simple, concrete, colorful world. And once you left the hospital, you had experienced something more than just sickness, and you actually had something to talk about. That was important as well.

Of course, the ergo therapists and occupational therapists were not the only ones who had this skill, who could see things for what they were, not what should have been, and to see that even though much is diseased, there can still be some good left. The male nurse was also one of them; the doctor who apologized was another. Humans that were just humans, in addition to being health professionals, and who accepted that I was a human being as well, in addition to being a patient. There were nurses who took walks with me and discussed things other than the disease, who loaned me books or music tapes, who took me to the movies, and who related to me as a normal, competent human being, even when everything seemed quite hopeless. They didn't necessarily try to change me, at least not all the time; they accepted that I was crazy or not crazy. There was the nurse who brought me a crossword puzzle when I was in the isolation room and he was shadowing me. He had been told not to speak to me; nobody was supposed to speak to me or answer what time it was or what was for dinner because I was supposed to have calm. I sat there for ten weeks, and I was starting to lose it completely because of the calm—too much calm borders on torture—and I longed for anything that was not calm. For instance, crosswords. Because solving crosswords is not talking, and pointing to answers cannot be described as a conversation. There was no law against nurses bringing reading materials, and most of them did. And many of them solved crossword puzzles. The difference was that he invited me over so that we could solve the puzzle together. Of course I was not always capable of solving the puzzle—sometimes I was too deep in my mess to see a single key word—but that was fine. The next time he tried again. Because that's life. Sometimes you have meat, sometimes you have pebbles, and sometimes only sand. I always liked the practitioners who accepted that life was like that and who wouldn't leave when I didn't have the sirloin. Because I never did.

The next person Askeladden met was a man who was suck- ing on a barrel tap. He was so thirsty that he could never drink enough, and since he didn't have the barrel, he had to be happy with the tap. He didn't even need pebbles; he could manage by sucking on the tap that wasn't connected to anything. Such things impress me. My first two therapists managed the same thing, and I thought it was quite admirable. They stuck with me for years, just as attentive, just as interested, just as engaged, even though they never got a drop in return. I never really got better; I never developed in any direction. If anything I got worse, but they stood by me. They gave me appointments, they came to responsibility group meetings, and they adjusted offers I was unable to manage. They didn't need feedback on whether or not this worked; they never threw the tap away and said that they were done, that we are getting nowhere. No, they continued, no matter what.

The ideal, in psychological health care as in every other area of health care, is to heal the patient. But that doesn't mean that it's not important to keep the patient alive, even without heal- ing. If I had managed to kill myself, all later attempts to heal me would have been useless. When the patient is dead, all hope is out. Therefore priority number one is to keep the person alive. And they did. They had conversation upon conversation with me, they had me admitted, they were there when I needed them, and they stuck by me. For years. And if they were tired of me, they hid it well; they had great patience and equal forbearance. They were there. Maybe they expected too little—maybe they didn't see all the opportunities present. Maybe they were part of systems that weren't so good and that they couldn't change, but they tried to minimize the damage nonetheless. And so what? I was there, I experienced them, and I experienced the systems. The world is sometimes unbelievably cruel not only to patients, but also to health professionals. I know that they did their very best, that they tried with their entire hearts and for many years. Maybe they couldn't break the system's curse, but they could lessen its effect, and they could keep me alive. They sucked that barrel tap eagerly for years, as if they were convinced that the nectar would suddenly flow out. And they did so even though both they and I could see that there was no longer a barrel to tap into. They didn't need a barrel, but they still kept hoping. What more can you really ask of a travel companion?

Some people can't hear you even if you are shouting in their ears. Others hear what you say as long as you speak clearly and directly, and as long as you give concrete messages of what you need. That's fine, but when I was sick, I was far from clear and direct; I was pretty confused, and I don't think my messages were always so easy to understand. "The ability to communicate is disturbed during psychosis," it is said, and even though it sounds terribly arrogant on the professional tongue, it is still true. It is hard to give clear messages when your head is full of knots and you can't understand your own thoughts and emotions, much less what other people try to express. Askeladden's third helper was so focused that he could hear the grass grow. I've met a lot of people who've been so focused that they could hear what was never said. People who assume that they will hear something meaningful and who therefore stop to listen instead of quickly moving on because it is impossible to hear the grass grow or to get something meaningful out of psychotic babble. Grass grows quietly, and you have to really listen if you want to hear it, but grass also grows slowly, so you need to take your time. Unfortunately, it is not very popular in modern health care to take the time to hear the grass grow. Everything moves fast and effectively, and they count measures and capacity and patient output. It is good to remove inefficiency and procrastination, but it is not as good when you push processes that can't be pushed.

Sometimes the pressure from the waiting list outside the door is so strong that it's painful to be inside. My therapists took their time. A lot of time. And it took years, and many therapy sessions, to get well, because change and insight is a process that has to grow from within and can't be hurried. The first two therapists gave me time and stuck by me even when it looked hopeless. When the time was right, I met the third who gave me room to develop into a full-fledged plant. Insight and health can't be given directly, just like you can't pull a sunflower out of a seed. But sunflower seeds won't blossom in your bag, either. They need space, earth, water, light, and nurturing to develop from a small hard core to a light flower. They need the opportunity for growth and care. You can give that, and I got it. I got time, safety, and space. I was allowed to explore my symptoms and my images of room, which felt safe with a travel companion who listened so well that we could hear the grass grow together. She listened, really listened, to the grass, and so I did as well, because it was suddenly allowed and even encouraged. And so I heard what the grass was saying, and we figured out the wolves and self-injury and the Captain and everything else out together. I didn't receive any final answers, but I did get the dirt to grow my own. That was the best part.

Askeladden's fourth helper was a man who had such good sight that he could see the end of the world. When Askeladden met him, he was just standing there, gazing, and I can imagine that he looked rather stupid. Because what's the point in seeing the end of the world? If you want to see far, you should look toward a goal within reach, something reasonable and that you realistically may reach. Or maybe not. Because the point of seeing the end of the world is, of course, that you practice your sight, and you become more awake and used to seeing farther.

At one point I met a rehabilitation counselor who dared to look toward the end of the world. She believed in my dreams even though they were wild, but at the same time she maintained a healthy realism and made us plan a safety net just in case. I had a few therapists who dared to look to the end of the world and who did this with the most natural platitude, as if it was the

least they could do. I also met others—caregivers, support coun-
selors, employees of public offices, my doctor—people who stood
up straight, lifted their gaze and looked far, much farther than
normal, when I asked them to. That was important. But first and
foremost I had my family. My mother and my sister, who refused
to accept how sick I was and who always looked forward no matter how bad my condition was. Every time I gave up and either
tried to kill myself, was admitted before I managed to try, or just
broke all together after a psychosis, my sister would sigh and say,
"Come now, it's going to be all right. I know that you are far out
on the wrong field, and now you got yourself in a hole as well, but
that's okay. This is just a small detour, and soon you will find your
way back to the road." Every single time. For about ten years. And
despite the fact that she was sometimes disappointed, she always
said the same thing: "Okay, so you got lost again. It is just a detour, come on, just continue, you will get there eventually." For ten
years. And when I got my diploma as a psychologist, she traveled
from Stavanger to Oslo to make sure that I had really reached my
goal and to be with me as I crossed the finish line. In her suitcase
she brought a picture for me. It was a picture of all the roads I
had taken, with all the nooks and turns. Up on the mountain,
down the cliff, out in the swamp, into the woods, a little up, a little
down, and back and forth, then in a cave and up over a hill. And,
lastly, at the finish line. It doesn't matter if you get lost a bit as long
as you know where you are going and you have the strength to
keep going the whole way. One of the reasons I had the strength
was that I always look forward and never gave myself permission
to give up, at least not for more than twenty-four hours at a time.
And if I gave up anyway, they wouldn't give up; they remained.
"Just as small detour, it will get better. Come on." How could I
give up then?

When I was in the closed ward and not allowed to have sharp
objects. I painted a lot, because you can do that with water, paper,
and a brush; these objects are not dangerous. I painted watercolors

because watercolors are usually nontoxic. Many of the paintings are sad, symbolic expressions of how I was feeling, but some are just paintings. There was a large one of a Christmas star against a dark-blue background. The painting was carefully done, I spent a lot of time on it, and it turned out quite nicely. The ergo therapist helped me make a frame out of black cardboard, and we hung it up on the wall. "You'll need to get a gold frame for this at some point and hang it over the coach in your living room," my mother said, who knew that I had no couch, no living room, no house, no exit, no income, and no ability to be in the same room as glass objects. She had attended multiple informational sessions where she had been told what was realistic to expect and what was unrealistic, but I don't think she listened very well. Now I have both a couch and a living room, and the picture hangs where she said it should, over the couch in my living room. In a golden frame. When you look to the end of the world, it's not problematic. She could see so clearly that she saw what was yet to come, and once she could do that, she increased the chances of it coming true. And it did.

The second to last passenger on Askeladden's ship was so light on his feet that he needed seven weights on his legs so that he wouldn't fly to the heavens. He might not have been able to spot the end of the world, but he could run there and back in less than five minutes if necessary, and he did it gladly. When the king wanted tea-water from the water source at the end of the world, he would be on his way immediately. Yes, he did fall asleep along the way, but with the help of the others, he got back to the royal palace with the water before his time was up. When I think that he, or his relatives, most likely worked at multiple public offices in my municipality and other places, too, I'm sure some people may protest. It is a common perception that employees in the public sector are square bureaucrats who try to make things as difficult as possible, and that public offices are places where everything takes way too long and humanity and efficiency is dead. This perception does not coincide with my experience, however.

I received meetings with psychologists for years, and they helped me. But these conversations, at least for some years, would never had happened if the case worker in social services had not recognized the importance of my having therapy and agreed to cover some of the charges.

Other helpers sat at the municipality's housing office and helped me get a state loan for an apartment where I could feel safe and where I could have the space to develop myself further. The loan also helped me enter the housing market so that later I could sell the apartment, pay the mortgage, and move onward on my own, on regular terms. The caseworkers were an important part to an indispensible springboard when I took off to get out into the world again.

Then others sat in the health care department as support contacts, home help, psychiatric nurses, and others who would help when the world got too rough, or they would be a buffer against the crushing loneliness. Some also worked in these services.

The last travel companion Askeladden met was the man who had swallowed fifteen winters and seven summers. I have no idea why he had swallowed fifteen winters exactly—fifteen is not a typical fairytale number—but it does occur to me that he ate twice as many cold and winter storms as he did summer warmth and spring breeze. He was the person that finally saved the crew, when it got really warm around them, and that makes sense to me. The ability to store everything is not a common trait, but it is important. Sometimes it is conclusive. I have met very few of his kind, but I've met some. People who have enough room, and enough inner strength, to accept, bear, and stand among all of the larger emotions. People who don't shy away when it storms, but who deal with anger, rage, bitterness, sorrow, shame, guilt, jealousy, joy, anxiety, longing, and love. Who accept the winter storms and welcome the summer warmth, and who have twice the amount of space for rough winter weather that they have for sun and drizzle.

When I was a teenager and I could tell that the dragon was swallowing me, I wrote in my diary that no matter what, I still wanted to paint with all the colors in my color palette. And even though I didn't know then how much it would take, I meant what I said. Unfortunately I learned that there are people, also in health care, who don't agree with me or Bjornson, and who think, rather, that calm is the ideal. And that you can't paint with all the colors. They meet strong emotions with fear and medications, to lessen the stronghold and to make the blood red pastel once more. Sometimes it was necessary, for a period of time, to look after me and to lighten a pain that would have been too large to handle. But in the long run it doesn't solve anything. Huge emotions can be violent, powerful, terrifying, and painful, but they are usually not dangerous. They may lead to dangerous actions—that's true—if they get out of control and if you are too scared of them, but the feelings, in themselves, are not dangerous. I realized this after a while, and I learned it from people who were not scared of emotions, their own or others', and who had room to carry them, embrace them, and then let them go, controlled, a little at a time. They showed, though actions and acceptance, that emotions are a good thing, and they taught me to paint with all the colors in a way that gave nice pictures and not just a mess. That wasn't just important—it was vital.

Sometimes it takes so little. This one nurse started every evening shift by entering the common room where I was sitting, going to the middle of the floor, then bending forward so that her upper body was horizontal, with one leg stretched out behind her, her weight resting on the other, and both of her arms elegantly stretched out to the sides. In this position she made flapping movements with her arms, before she straightened back up. When people asked what she was doing, she always answered the same thing: "I'm just flying for Arnhild, since she misses flying so badly." She had seen the drawings in my room where I had written: "Only caged birds long for something. Free birds fly." She saw that I missed flying. She saw that the cage bothered me. She knew that I thought in literal terms and that actions could have great symbolic meaning for me. So she started her evening shifts by flying. It took her about one minute. And during that minute she showed me that she saw me, that she accepted my dreams and my wants, that she accepted my way of expressing myself, and that she wanted to help me keep my dream alive.

I am aware that there is a crisis in psychological health care. I know that we have great, pervasive problems that can only be solved through more money and comprehensive structural changes. I know that many systems are damaging and should be reorganized. But I also know that behind the money and systems there are people. And sometimes the people can change the systems completely. Sometimes they can better the systems a little or they can lessen the bad side effects the system gives to people. And sometimes all they can do is fly. It may seem tiny and unimportant. It doesn't change anything in the long run. It is not important, necessary, or big. But it felt good. It gave me hope. That nurse may have wanted to change the system if she could, but she couldn't, not then. But she could fly. So she flew. And I loved it.

Canes, crutches, and fences

If you own a couple of proper canes there are multiple ways you can use them. You can make a fence to lock people or animals in, you can use them as support or as crutches if someone is hurt or if the ground is uneven, or you may use them to beat people you don't like or don't agree with—among other things. And medications are the same. Used in the proper way, medications can be a good support that makes the symptoms more manageable, and they can ease the pain somewhat so that people gain the strength to go on living. They can also dampen bothersome voices and lessen the effects of the disease, like self-injuring and other forms of acting out, so that people may function better in their everyday lives.

But medications can also be a fence, with dulling results and side effects that trap people in a diseased state and keep them from moving on with active therapeutic transformation work, while removing the strength that would make them healthy. And as I said before, the topic of "medications" is very current in the type of discussions that concern being right and convincing your opponents that there is only one truth, namely the one I have—that the most important function of a cane is that it's an okay weapon. During the past years I've traveled a lot, and I've met a lot of patients and dependents. Some, actually many, strongly opposed the use of medications and react strongly to how people in crisis are not offered another kind of help instead of medications to deal with their lives. They are often outspoken, and often pretty angry, and many have a line of bad experiences that gives them good reason to be opposed to medication. Others are happy with the use of medications. They say that it helps them in everyday life, and they say that they've accepted the fact that this is a necessity for them. Many of them have tried to go off the medications multiple times, and every time they experience relapses, defeat, and chaos. They are often a tad bit more quiet, and I sometimes perceive them as ashamed—they haven't "succeeded" in quitting the medications, and thus they are not as "good" as the ones that did "succeed." And this is, of course, not true.

A while back I wanted to try to create a small overview of my life using dates. I was starting to tire of having to count my way back and forth to figure out when I started school, which year I started my studies, when I was admitted for the first time, and so on, so I thought that a chronological overview would be a good thing to have. It went fine in the beginning. I know when I was born, when my father died, when I started the first grade. I also remember when I began high school and when I was admitted for the first time, and I could also remember what happened and which institutions I lived in during the years right after this. But then it stops. So I started counting backward instead. I know where I live and work right now, and I could work my way backward without too much trouble find out when I finished my studies, when I moved into my house, when I started at the university, when I attended adult education, and when I got my diploma. For a while it all went smoothly, but then it stopped again. Finally I had to give up, and for a couple of years, in the beginning of my twenties, it simply says "slept." Because that was what I was doing. These are years I haven't shared stories about, and that I rarely or never talk about in my lectures. Not because they are so terrible that I can't talk about them, but because there is nothing to say. I slept. I had been in and out of hospitals for years, I had gone through a lot of self-injuring and acting out, and I was simply in a lot of pain. To lessen the pain and make it possible for me to live outside of the ward, I received medications, a lot of medications, the old-fashioned kind of neuroleptics, and then I slept. I lived at home with my mother, and she took care of all of the practicalities: food, chores, and so on. I would get out of bed in the afternoon, I think, get dressed, and eat. After this I was so tired that I went back to bed, and then I slept for a few hours. Then I got back up, chatted with my mother, maybe I sat in the yard for a while if the weather was nice, maybe I listened to some music, and then I went back to bed. On Saturdays my mother would drive me to a mall so that I could see some people, but we were never gone for long. I didn't have the strength. I was still in therapy, and even though a taxi drove me back and forth, I was always exhausted afterward. I don't think the therapy was very helpful. I slept. I was rarely awake for more than a three hours at a time, I do remember that. And that was the issue, and the important reason why I rarely talk about these years: I don't remember them. I remember everything else, even the things that were painful, but I can't remember this.

It can sometimes be confusing to remember things that happened when I was very psychotic because things don't make sense; it is almost like thinking back on a dream, or something that happened when you were very little—the memories are strange and illogical because they stem from situations when the brain was illogical and organized differently. But these years are different. The memories aren't strange, they are just gone. I remember some things, barely, and the rest I have to ask others about, the ones who surrounded me at the time. These are lost years. Years that are stolen from my history, but that still, as the blank holes they are, are also part of my history. A history with holes.

Even though I was severely drugged, my symptoms never completely disappeared. I know that it was often difficult for my mom to deal with me at home. She doesn't talk about it much, but when I ask, she says some, and then I remember a little bit myself as well. I tried to run away a couple of times, but I have no idea what I thought that would be good for. I may have been concerned, scared, or uncomfortable, and I know that the voices bothered me somewhat. They never fully disappeared, even though there were periods when I didn't care much about what they said. I was admitted a couple of times when things got too hard, and I complained that I was scared and worried. I had never complained about that before. I am not easily scared, but I was frightened then. Maybe because somewhere within me I did register that there was no real life left in me—maybe because the blend of medications gave me side effects that included restlessness and worrying, maybe something else. I don't know. But I know that I was scared a lot. And I know that I often, almost compulsory, repeated, "I want to go home. I am scared, I want to go home." Obviously, my mother didn't like this much because I would say this even when I was physically at home, but I understand it well now, in retrospect. I had gotten lost in the fog. I had lost myself, my stubbornness, my dreams, my will, and my vivaciousness. It scared me, and I wanted to go back home to the "me" I knew. They say that "you can never have my thoughts" and "your thoughts are free, who do you think it will find. It flies by, like shadows disappear." I sang this song when I was sitting in isolation, and when I was sitting in a foster position at the fenced porch, with a roof, at the hospital. And I loved the rebellious feeling I got from the lines: "And if we are forced behind ironclad doors, then the wind will escape, that transports the thoughts." But during the years I slept, I didn't sing. My rebellious spirit was dulled down, my thoughts were locked up, and my will entrapped. And I slept.

While I am writing this, I also know that I was in a lot of pain, and that I actually hurt myself quite a lot. The alternative to heavy medications would have been a continued stay at a good institution, and good, well run, long-term institutions with focus on both care and treatment are hard to come by. Besides, I had been admitted for so long, maybe it was good for me to be outside for a while. I know that it's not healthy to be on such heavy medications—nothing in the world can make me say that it was good for me. Never. But at the same time, I also realize that there were few good or achievable alternatives at that time. They were bad years, and not healthy or educational in any way, and I was lucky to get out the other end without any lasting damage from the large drug doses, I know that. It wasn't good. But I survived.

After a couple of years like this, the group in charge of me decided that it was time to move on. I was relatively calm now, and even though I was dulled down, I still had some will left. I was enrolled in an introductory class in arts and crafts, under specific conditions and with an assistant. The setup was very good. I got a taxi to drive me back and forth and an assistant during classes, and I only went for half a day at the time. They had considered many elements. That's because educators, psychologists, and caseworkers set it up, but medications are the business of doctors and had nothing to do with education. I was still supposed to take my medications, and I would still go to school, and these were two completely separate things. But I was one person. And the same medications that made me calm enough to attend school, and that dulled my hallucinations enough so that I could hear the teacher also made me so hung over and tired that it was difficult to attend school. And they largely affected my fine motor skills. Ever since my teenage years I had kept a journal, at least in periods, and when I go through my journals I can easily see how my handwriting changed from my own to the medicated handwriting and back to my own. My handwriting hasn't changed much from when I was eighteen, but there are great differences between the handwriting I had when I was medicated and the one I have when I am drug-free.

I can remember that medication affected a lot of other things in my life as well. I chose sneakers with Velcro because it was so tiresome to tie my shoelaces. I stopped eating grilled chicken, which I really like, because it was so difficult to remove the meat from the bones with a knife and fork. I generally struggled with the knife and fork, and I preferred stews and other foods that were easy to consume. And in this state I started arts and crafts classes. My handwriting was terrible, and the calligraphy classes were a disaster. My creativity had gone to bed, and my hands hurt as much as they could, and yet there were no apparent results. I struggled with drawing, knitting, painting, and weaving, and anything that demanded even the smallest physical effort made me exhausted, like felting. And because I liked all of these things and thought they were fun, I was sad when I couldn't do them properly. I wasn't aware that this was all a side effect of my medications. It seems unfathomable that I didn't realize, but I didn't. Maybe because I was too sick, maybe I was too dulled down, maybe I just didn't have the knowledge. Maybe I didn't think about it.

When I read my journal, I can see that the content was affected, just as much as the handwriting. During the periods when I could find the strength to write, the content was flat, banal, and pretty embarrassing. They are not well written, and there's a lack of imagery, glow, and reflection. You can't have a heart without the ache, and I have accepted my disease. I don't read these notes often; they are just sad and embarrassing. I clearly didn't think much when I was writing, and maybe I didn't think much when I wasn't writing either. I can't really remember. But I know that I didn't see the connection between the medication and the challenges I was having, and I know that because I remember so well when I finally discovered the connection. That was many years later. Back then I didn't see it, but I did see that I managed poorly and that everything I made turned out badly and that it was no longer fun. That made me sad and scared, and I said this. I lost the will to go to school—I was scared to go. But school was an important part of the rehabilitation that people had put a lot of work into, and it was important to get me to follow through with it. So, I was encouraged to continue, and I was given more medications if I needed it. I did. My handwriting got even worse, and I got even more scared, and my daily doses were increased again. And again. But it didn't help, because no one saw the connection and nobody understood that what had been done to improve the situation actually made it worse. After a few months I was finally admitted. I tried to go back to school once I was released, but I was only admitted again. I never finished the introductory class.

Looking at this from the outside, this may seem like a failed attempt to rehabilitate a schizophrenic patient who eventually proved to be too sick to rehabilitate, even with extensive facilitation. I was on the inside, and I don't think it was only me and the disease that made it all go wrong. I think the attempt was doomed to fail from the beginning, because medical expertise was not involved in the formation of the plans. And I am not talking about a doctor saying, "Okay, I will take care of the prescriptions and then you take care of the education"—but a person that knows, really knows, the side effects of the specific medications and who would assess the effects they had on me in particular. There might have been a different outcome with such collaboration between the educators and doctors. They might have decided to delay the attempt, or they might have decided on a different program that had less to do with my motor skills. They could have tried to put me on another kind of drug instead that would have given fewer of the side effects that were least wanted in this situation. And, if nothing else, they could have explained the situation to me and informed me that the bad results had nothing to do with me but were a result of the medications instead. It wouldn't have changed much, but at least we might have avoided the increased dosage. And after a while I could maybe have been secure enough to decrease the doses. Maybe. Either way, such collaboration might have prevented the public sector spending money on a hopeless project, and I wouldn't have felt like a complete failure, even failing at the things I had been able to do all my life. Furthermore, I would not have received "rehabilitation failed" noted in my journal, which looked like a result of disease, but that was really a result of treatment.

One of the great dangers of taking medication is that over time, while the disease develops and the caretakers are exchanged, the initial problems are forgotten and the symptoms and side effects are suddenly confused. After I got well, one of my therapists, who followed me for a long time and knew me well, told me that she had seen that I was getting sicker, and that the psychosis made me dull, quiet, and less open to therapy. That frightened me. It was true it happened, but it wasn't the psychosis that did it. The medications were supposed to fight the psychosis. And that's not the same thing.

Another danger is the outer stigma of being a psychiatric patient becomes even worse when you are struggling with obvious side effects that actually make you look funny. I gained a lot of weight while I was medicated, twenty to thirty kilograms, that disappeared again when I was off the drugs. My facial expressions were reduced, and I felt like my face was no longer alive, that it was a mask. My movements were stiff and impaired, both my rough and fine motor skills were affected, my arms no longer moved when I walked, and I walked heavily. It was tiresome to move, and it always felt like walking in water, no matter where I walked. I know that physical activity is healthy when you are psychologically sick, but I also know that it can be very hard to move your body when it is packed with drugs.

When I started to realize what the medications were doing to me and what was going on, I had wild fantasies about how some top athlete would take a couple of doses of neuroleptics and then try to finish a race, as a demonstration. I thought that this might make the nurses understand that it wasn't about laziness or lack of motivation or will power, and that there was therefore no reason to yell at me when I didn't want to go for a walk—I was just exhausted. My body was affected by the medications I took to affect my body, something that wasn't really strange and it wasn't my fault—I wanted to—but I couldn't. They thought it was me, but it wasn't. It was the medication.

This is very obvious today, when I am not medicated, because now I'm me again. I sleep for six to eight hours each night, a little bit more if I'm tired, but never fifteen or seventeen. I have shoes with laces, I often think and reflect, and I like crafts. I know that I've been lucky. I have had very few delayed effects after the years on medication. As a student we used to rehearse with each other when we were learning about various topics, and it made me suspicious that my fine motor skills are still not what they should be. I also know that I commonly drop small things, like screws, on the ground before I am able to screw them into the wall, but it doesn't keep me from making small repairs around the house and from continuously exploring new craft techniques. My handwriting is back, as are my facial expressions and my ability to reflect. I can feel cold and warmth, and I have sensitive skin. I am completely free of drugs, and I've been for many, many years, and I know that this was the best solution for me. Because now, I'm myself again.

At the same time I know that it may not be the best solution for everyone. People vary. We have different beginnings, different challenges, and different goals. Age, disease, and length of disease vary, and for some, using large or small doses of medications for shorter or longer periods of time is the right thing to do. I also know that the old neuroleptics, which I used, are now rarely prescribed, and that the new drugs have different side effects. But there are still side effects. It scares me when I hear drug representatives saying that "this drug may cause chest pains and milk production in the patient, that may be uncomfortable for a man, but for a woman it may not matter." Oh no? I lactated because of some of my medication, and it was very uncomfortable, and it made me scared because I didn't understand what was happening to me. I never asked my doctor either, even though there was a doctor at the institution once a week—an elderly, serious, man—but I would have never thought to talk to him about the spots on my clothes. It ended after a while, but it was scary and absolutely not preferred. Even though I'm a woman, I don't want to lactate when I am not pregnant and there's no baby that needs the milk. It does matter. And it mattered when I was a patient.

And so it is not the drugs themselves I'm skeptical of. I know, from experience, that in certain periods it can be good to use medication to dampen the worst outbreaks of the disease and to make life manageable. Sometimes you need something to take off the edge of pain that would otherwise be unbearable. Sometimes you are so tired that a chemical solution is the only manageable solution. I also know, very well, that all patients are different, and that for some patients, in some situations, medication is the best solution and may be the only solution. Sometimes, it is also the solution people want, even though other, more painful solutions, can work as well. I have tried the painful road myself, and I don't think we should demand that of anyone. But they should have a real choice. They should have information. And as a health practitioner you should evaluate the situation, including the medications, and not demand something of the patients that the medications prohibit them from successfully doing. We should also remember that when we see a heavily medicated person, that's not the entire picture, but only a piece of the picture. And first and foremost, we should maintain their respect and humility. Because even though the side effects may be necessary right there and then, they are never wanted, and it is never "okay." Schizophrenics are human beings as well.

Lastly: Medications can, for some, have serious downsides and side effects. Still, you should never quit them cold turkey. It can be very dangerous and may enhance the injuries. Medications affect the chemical balance of the brain—that's the reason why you take them—and if you quit too quickly and the chemical influence on the brain stops too abruptly, it may lead to a lot of chaos and may exacerbate your condition. In addition, it can be dangerous in a strictly physical way. Therefore, it is best to talk to a doctor before you go off the medications. That way, you can get answers to your questions, and if it's a wise doctor, one you trust, you may get help to find the solution that's best for your specific situation. Maybe it is best that you change to a different drug, with different side effects. Maybe you need more information about what you are on, about the side effects, and a conversation about the upsides and downsides of this exact medication. Maybe you can try to decrease your doses, slowly and with control, either to reduce the side effects somewhat or to go off the drug completely. The solutions will vary because people vary. I am not saying that all patients should go off medication. In the long run, I wish that were possible, but I want to be realistic, and I don't think it is. But I still don't think that it is a necessity that all patients with schizophrenia have to use medications for the rest of their lives. That's to say, I know it is not a necessity, because I've experienced it.

Stop the world—I want to get back on!

"Stop the world—I want to get off!" we sometimes say in Norway, and this has long been illogical to me. It's not very hard to jump off a moving train. Of course you'll be bruised, you will be battered and dazed and injured, but you will get off. You need only look around a little bit and you see it everywhere, an increasing number of people jumping—or falling—off a world that keeps moving faster and faster (much like a train) and that continues to demand more of the people who want to stay on. No, it's easy enough to fall off. It is getting back on, while in motion, that's the problem, and for too many people, their attempts lead only to disappointment and bruises. They can't do it, and so they assume that they lack certain abilities, but they don't. It is simply very hard to jump on anything that's moving at a high speed without it ending badly. What you need is a vessel that you can get on while it is standing still and that gradually increases the speed with the passengers onboard until it's keeping the same speed as the world, and you can get on without jeopardizing life and health, almost like the system they use to fill gas in the tank of a flying aircraft. It is possible,but it demands a little care, facilitation, and planning.

The first thing you need to know is when to begin planning and where you want to go. I wanted to get completely healthy, and I wanted a degree as a psychologist, which was my goal. But many of the helpers around me saw how sick I was, and so instead they wanted me to work toward more realistic goals: that I would become more independent and learn to live with my symptoms. These goals were fine, but they didn't inspire me to fight. Lack of motivation, they would say, as if there was something wrong with me, and that it was impossible to motivate me because I generally lacked motivation. That wasn't true. I was motivated for many things, but like most people, I didn't like all things the same. I didn't want to go to the North Pole, I didn't want to become a composer, I didn't want to learn how to live with my symptoms—I wanted to become a psychologist. Since the latter was completely impossible and unrealistic, the helpers around me quickly dismissed this aspiration—it didn't motivate them, and so we chose their plan. Or, that is to say, they went for their plan. I didn't contribute much. But that wasn't surprising, for I was sick, and it was impossible to expect anything of me at all.

After a while they started arranging a series of initiatives, with varying results, and I never felt like they brought me much closer to my goal. One therapist did one thing, the other something else, and it was never easy to see the purpose of it all. This may be because none of the people around me really believed in my dream, or that it was possible for me to achieve it, so it was difficult for them to jostle up any real effort to help me move forward.

But they did try. I got work training. I was rolling earplugs in the workroom. The work was basically cutting small parts of pink, clay-like material, weighing them accurately—I am pretty sure they were supposed to weight exactly five grams—and then rolling them into pretty and even marbles. The marbles were places in boxes, two marbles per box. I got paid as well, five Kroners per work session I finished. I didn't finish many of them. And then the therapists got even more convinced of their opinion and thought that a person who couldn't even finish such simple work had to realize that the dream of studying at a university was completely unrealistic. But in this calculation they forgot one important element: desire. I didn't want to roll earplugs. I found it extremely boring, and I didn't see the point. I am capable of doing boring things, but they should have a purpose, and I saw no purpose with the plugs, not for me at least. I didn't learn anything new, I didn't move forward, and it didn't help me get closer to my goal. They said that I wasn't motivated. I knew that rolling earplugs didn't motivate me. Those aren't the same thing.

At that time there were some reorganization and legal changes that affected my local social security office. The responsibility of distributing the welfare checks was moved from the social security administration to another agency, and I got a new caseworker. I had been on welfare for quite some time, but now I had to change from medicinal welfare to unemployment pay, and we were expected to have a plan. Since I was not easily transported, my caseworker came to visit me at the hospital, and we were supposed to make a plan. She had to come to me, since I couldn't get to her, and she met a heavily drugged patient who, despite the medications, was still hallucinating and injuring herself and who couldn't go outside on her own and couldn't live by herself, who had no education past high school and who couldn't roll earplugs or keep up with the arts and craft class, who heard voices daily and who said she wanted to be a psychologist. I still wonder what I would have done in the same situation. I hope that I would have been able to believe the person, but I'm not completely convinced. In any case, she believed in me, and that day we wrote a plan with a university degree as the goal. Completely insane. But still, we now had a new plan, and for the first time since I got sick, and that was many years before this, we had a plan that actually propelled me toward my goal. Where I had always wanted to go. And it made a world of difference.

The plan was ambitious. Very ambitious. To reduce the chance of failure, and so that we could defend the plan, we had a plan B and alternative plans. Since I didn't have a high school diploma, I had to first obtain that. And to further my chances at the university, we combined the high school diploma with an introductory course in health and social care. That was smart. First off, these classes interested and motivated me and kept me focused on working toward my dream. Second, the introductory course worked as a nice safety net. If it happened that I was unable to continue studying, then I could at least finish the course and still become an occupational therapist, which could also give me a good life. And if I never got healthy enough to manage a job, I could just live in an apartment with supervision and work a few hours a week in a communal-adapted profession, at a workroom or a home for the elderly, or something similar. And that would be a good life as well, at least a lot better than the one I had. And so the plan was perfect. It was motivating, because it was helping me to realize my dream, and it was also safe, because I wouldn't lose it all if I didn't reach the top. Genius. And then, when the plan was ready and we were finally moving in the same direction, the work could begin.

In the beginning it was quite slow. We moved forward, but with tiny steps. I was still living in the institution, but a teacher from the high school close by came to see me a couple of times a week and educated me. We started with Norwegian, since I liked that class; we read textbooks and I wrote some assignments. I had home economics as well, with a different teacher. This was categorized as ADL training, or training in Activities for Daily Life, but in reality it meant that we were in a kitchen at the ward and made food. And I even participated in real classes, as a visiting student, for two hours each week. Despite the slow start, it demanded a lot more of me than the earplugs I was used to rolling, but I continued to do better. And even though I was terrified to walk into the new class—and it had been ages since I was in a classroom with other students—I did it. I had a worthwhile goal to push for and it was fine that I had to work hard to achieve it.

After a few months with careful education, that spring we were almost ready for the next step: "regular" lessons at a regular school in a regular classroom. It was arranged that I would finish the introductory course over two years because a full school week was too much for me at the moment. Furthermore, I got an assistant who met me outside of the school and followed me inside, since I was too scared to do it on my own, and the assistant was also with me during all my classes. The greatest challenge for me at the time was not the curriculum; even though the medication made my brain slower that normal, the academic part was fine. But I was scared of the other students, scared of myself, and scared of the hallucinations and delusions that were still bothering me. My assistant was the safety net I needed to be able to walk into classes and stay there, and I learned to trust that she would help me master the challenges I would meet along the way.

During the first years of my schooling, I lived at the institution, walked the five-minute walk over to the school, had my classes, and then walked back. My assistant escorted me inside in the morning, and the staff from the institution escorted me back in the afternoons. Some of them were great support people who motivated me whether I was trying to do my homework or just trying to get out of the door in the morning. And it went pretty well. I had a new therapist, and I was given a lot of support and a lot of knowledge through my sessions with her. I received help to rent an apartment in my home municipality, and after a careful transitional phase, I was released from the hospital in the beginning of the summer. The municipality was not ready for me, despite the fact that they had been warned in plenty of time, so the summer was hard, but I got through, and in fall I was starting the second half of my introductory course at the same school as before, with the same assistant. There was only one small problem. The school and institution were at Eidsvoll. My home municipality was Lorenskog—about 70 kilometers away. Obviously, I had no car or driver's license. This meant that I, still partly psychotic and still heavily medicated, had to take the bus to Lillestrom, then wait there for the train to Edsvoll, then take another bus from the station to the bus terminal, and then walk up the hill to the school. Today, that last walk would take me about ten minutes. Back then, with the medications, though, it took at least thirty minutes. The whole trip, therefore, took between one and two hours. Each way. I have no idea how anyone would ever think this would work out. And it didn't work out.

When I fell into psychosis again, I was admitted. My diagnosis was still genetic vulnerability and schizophrenia, and even though I obviously don't know what people were thinking, I do not recall anyone saying anything about the fact that my days were much too demanding, considering my condition. Because only a year had passed since nothing was demanded of me, and now people were suddenly demanding everything. No wonder the Captain lost it, for demands were his specialty—and since there was no connection between the therapy's "you have to take care of yourself and you should set boundaries" and the daily school, living, loneliness, bus, and train demands, it was only natural that the warning light went off.

Besides, my dream wasn't very motivating just then because I had never been healthy—as an adult, that is—and I didn't know how that felt. I was young when I got sick, and this was my first time living on my own and going to school and living a "normal" life. And to be honest, I didn't like it at all at first. So if this was "good," well, then maybe it wasn't worth the fight. Therapy demanded a lot of me, the buses demanded a lot, and the weekends and nights in my apartment were so endlessly lonely. Nothing was fun anymore. And because I still hadn't been far enough removed from my illness to see what was going wrong—that it was completely natural if my plans didn't work out—and because I still had more pictures than words and very few strategies for problem-solving, the psychosis came and saved me from a life that was crushing me. Obviously this was not good but it was the only available solution for me at the time. It got me into a ward away from the world, and it alerted those around me that the current system we'd set up wasn't working. And so we had to try again, with a new approach that would hopefully make it go smoother.

And we did. Again and again. The plans changed as we went; for instance, I dropped the health and social care course and went to GED classes instead. But the goal remained the same, even though I still gave up on occasion. Sometimes things went well, and other times not so well, and sometimes I didn't do anything at all.

Over the years I have gained a great respect for timing. Sometimes things just need to mature a bit before it's the right time for them to happen. I had tried to be successful at school before this as well; I had attended arts and crafts classes before I was moved to the earplug factory. My current plan was well intentioned but the timing was just not right. Even the best-tasting apple in the world was once sour.

One important part of therapy was that it gave me room to understand my symptoms and to mature more, so that the images and emotions began to have words and stopped being unmanageable images only. Another, equally important part of therapy was its role in helping me understand the world and my role in it. Because living for a long time at an institution or being part of a treatment plan does break you. Here's an example: At the institution, if I was sad and wanted contact and sat alone in a small nook of the common room, one of the staff members would usually approach me, ask what was wrong, and see if there was anything she could do for me. Outside of the ward, if I was feeling lonely or sad during a break in my adult education course, no one would come over and check in on me. This didn't necessarily mean that they didn't like me or wanted to hurt me, but it just meant that in the normal world, sitting on your own, away from everyone else, is usually a sign that you want to be left alone. This was a clear signal that I didn't know about, but that I could learn by going through such situations with my therapist and exploring alternative ways of receiving attention when I needed it.

The next step, which was a lot scarier, was that I needed to start implementing these alternative solutions, like sitting down at the table with the others in my class during the break, chatting about classes, school, and the weather, and seeing if it worked for me and if I felt respected and accepted by the others. It was scary in the beginning, but it got easier, because it actually worked. And in this way my therapist and I went through multiple situations, discussed them, and explored them, and then I experimented with new ways of reacting in the world, and the new solutions were evaluated. What worked well, what didn't work, what could I do differently, and so on. It was a lot of work, but it was effective. And a reason why it worked was simply that therapy became a parallel process to life; I had a life now and something to work on, I was motivated, and I had someone who helped me work on my life with me. Besides, the timing was also right. I was ready to move on.

I wanted to be healthy, but I couldn't fully picture what "healthy" meant right away. At one ward the staff used to ask the patients, during the morning meeting, the following question: "Do you really want to be healthy?" Usually this question came whenever the nurses were feeling discouraged by the patients' apparent lack of improvement, or if a particular patient didn't do as they wanted. "Do you really want to be healthy?" If the question were directed to me, I would always answer yes—what else could I say? But I didn't always feel honest answering in the affirmative. Because I wasn't sure if I really *did* want to be healthy all the time.

The Danish philosopher Søren Kierkegaard developed a thesis about the three stages a person can be in. He called the first stage the esthetic stage and described it as a condition dominated by want, esthetic, and joy. Choices are made based on what feels good, fun, or pretty, or whatever prevents boredom. It doesn't necessarily have to be physical enjoyment, but may also be art, entertainment—anything that makes sure that you are not bored. The next stage, which Kierkegaard views as honorable, is the ethic stage. Here you make decisions based on ethical values and evaluations; you make moral considerations, and you do your duty, even though it is boring. Humans in the ethical stage don't talk about "the beautiful" or "the good," and they don't write poetry about justice and truth—they go out and *do* good, even when it is tiresome or boring. Then there is the third and most honorable stage, according to Kierkegaard. This is the religious stage. This is also the most difficult stage, and according to Kierkegaard many people never achieve this. He describes this stage as like being in deep waters and describes the blind faith and trust in something you cannot see, cannot prove, but still act in accordance with—like Socrates emptying his cup of poison in blind faith in the invincibility of the soul, or Abraham who was willing to sacrifice his only son because he believed God's words.

Something about all this made me think of the frightening question the nurses would propose: Do you really want to be healthy? Blind faith was what I needed—to act, to do something difficult and disconcerting without proof that it was right and without guarantees that it would work right away. Blind faith. Without a shred of evidence. I will most likely never reach the last stage that Kierkegaard proposed, but I know that it was difficult in my very simplified version of life's many stages. It is hard to change careers halfway through. It doesn't get any easier by not knowing what you're walking toward, what you are really working so hard for, and if it's possible to ever achieve your goals.

This is difficult because the patient role is a career as well, and like all careers, it is built and developed over time. I had been sick for years—my entire adult life, actually, and large parts of my youth as well—and that was what I knew; that was my career. Large chunks of my life were built upon being in the patient role. I had a home because I was sick. I had an income—welfare—because I was sick. The social rules I knew were based on my disease, on what I did during the day; either I was in an institution, at a day center, or in rehabilitation, and this was because of my diagnosis. My social network, whether it was paid caretakers or inner voices, was there because of my illness. If I became healthy, I imagined that I would lose everything because I didn't have any other experiences, and I didn't know that I could attain so much more than what I had. I couldn't imagine, I couldn't even believe in it, but I still had to try. I had some courage, but not that much.

I believe in a good God, and I sometimes go to religious services. While I was still sick, we would pray for the other sick during our patient meetings. It would never occur to me to lead the prayer—I didn't dare—and besides, the mood was a bit too aggravated for me to be comfortable, but I prayed on my own, and I assumed that God could hear me no matter where I sat. Besides, I trusted that He could hear crazy prayers as well. I told Him that I would get healthy but that I was also terrified, and I asked Him to be nice and make me well again. But I also prayed that it would take awhile "because I am too scared of the fast pace." It did take a long time in the end. And no matter if you believe in God or not I'm sure you can relate to the feeling that even though disease is painful, it is also familiar and therefore safe. Luckily, I met a therapist who understood this and who told me that with my diagnosis, and with a journal as thick as the phonebook, it would take some time before I got healthy. This made me feel safe because it gave me time. Besides, it felt good to know that she could put my fears into words, especially since it is unfortunately common in the health care system that if you do as the therapists say and you get a little better, you lose the offer for treatments and are released, even though you don't feel healthy enough. It doesn't happen because most caretakers are evil or stupid but because the treatment offered to a patient is a treatment that someone else really needs as well, and because it's not always possible to think long-term. Luckily, it's not like that everywhere. In many places there's actually some room to give, at least some patients, what they need the most—a long follow-up. But the patient isn't necessarily aware of needing this. My experience as a patient was that I was always scared to lose my spot if I got better just a little bit, and my experience as a psychologist is that when I ask patients about this, I often receive answers that confirm that this is their fear as well. That's why I sometimes ask them what they are feeling. Not because it has to be true, but because it sometimes is. And it is easier to work together—both for the patient and for the health practitioner—if you can agree that the treatment will not end if it starts working.

The last time I was admitted to the hospital I had no idea that it would be my last time. At the time, I thought everything was over. It had been going well for a while; I had a part-time job; I was off the drugs; I had tried to do something sensible; and then all of a sudden I ended up back in the ward, in the belted bed. I wanted to give up. I saw no other solution, and I just wanted to die. The voices, confusion, fog, and sensory disturbance always managed to return. I always wound up in some chaos that I couldn't handle, until the belted bed handled it for me. It was useless, I thought, because I didn't know that this would be the last time. Many years went by before I realized that it was the last time, though. I never went back. But I didn't know that then.

What's considered important in life and treatment varies from person to person. To me it was important to work on becoming healthy. But that will not be what's important for all people, and it is vital for health care professionals and family members to remember that. When I got sick, I was told that my disease was chronic and that I would never be healthy again. That was repeated many times during my illness, and it was the reason why rolling earplugs may have seemed like a good job for someone like me. But it was never a good fit for me, and I know that the constant focus on hopelessness only damaged me. It is therefore important to me, as a therapist, to convey a sense of hope and to give my patients faith in numerous possibilities for their futures, even if a diagnosis is serious. I know that I would have appreciated receiving that hope when I was sick, and so I want to share it now.

I was immensely lucky to get healthy, and I am very grateful. That gratitude also contains understanding, respect, and humility toward those who receive larger burdens than I and who never get fully healthy. This is the way with many diseases. Some recover from cancer, some may live for a long time with the disease, and some die quickly. And this is also the case with schizophrenia. Some are bothered with symptoms their entire life, some die of suicide or accidents, some manage pretty well for periods of time, and some recover. And anyone who wants should be allowed to hope in a better future, no matter if that hope is realistic or not. Today, when we have the answer sheet, I could easily say that I was carrying the opportunity to recover. But it is when everything seems impossible that you need hope. Some dreams do come true. Some don't. When I was in high school, I wanted to be a psychiatrist, win at least one Nobel Prize, and dance in the ballet. I never became a dancer, and I will never receive a Nobel Prize. But I did become a psychologist. And I have a great life that I enjoy. There is no need for all of your dreams to come true in order to feel good. And hope should always be allowed, no matter if you are ill or not.

Gray as sheep, golden as a lion

Hans Christian Andersen's story about the ugly duckling that is teased by the other ducks but then grows up to become a beautiful swan is often paraphrased when written. In a children's book I had when I was a child, it read: "The winter was long and hard and the duckling was sad." One long winter, in only one sentence. In the original story, Andersen spends many pages on the same winter and explains how the duckling is fooled, exploited, and exposed to a variety of dangers. There is also a beautiful description of when the duckling freezes in the ice but is then saved by a nice farmer who takes him home and warms him in front of the fire. When the farmer's children want to play with him, he is scared that they will hurt him; he flies up, spills the milk bucket, and escapes out of the open door in complete chaos. It is not always easy to recognize kindness when the world has been evil for so long. When spring finally arrives, the duckling finds a pond with three beautiful swans in it. He admires them, but he also assumes that they will despise him—even kill him. Still, he thinks that it would be better to be killed by such beautiful birds than to suffer through another winter like this. Andersen's duckling doesn't swim over to the other swans because he hopes that they might accept him. He swims over to them and waits to be killed. In reality, he is making a suicide attempt. But he doesn't succeed. They don't kill him. And while he waits for them to act like he expected, he bows his head in shame and anxiety and sees his own reflection in the water. The others didn't kill him; they accepted him, and so he was able to discover that he had become a beautiful swan.

That's just the way it goes. When you've grown accustomed to a difficult world and have been told that you are useless, it can be hard to walk out into the world again and to turn all of the expectations for yourself, the world, and other people upside down. It can be pretty confusing that there is "light at the end of the tunnel"; this has become a tired cliché, and I can't count the number of times I've heard that even though it is dark now, there's light out there. It has always amazed me that drivers aren't told about the dangers of the glare from the sun when driving between light and dark places. It's a known fact that tunnel openings can cause accidents because you are easily confused by the transition from dark to bright daylight. That doesn't mean that it's not easier to drive in daylight, because it is; it just means that the transition might be too hard on your eyes.

Paid helpers surrounded me every day, for many years. For six or seven years of my life there was no one, except my closest family, who spent time with me for free, voluntarily, or without receiving payment. That did something to my self-image. Some of the paid helpers were arrogant, indifferent, or ruthless; the majority were not. Most of them showed me respect, understanding, and professionalism, or they tried to. Most of them wanted to build up my self-esteem, and many told me how much I was worth, that I was a good person, and so on. But it only helped so much. It didn't say much that nurses and therapists told me how great I was, when the truth was that they were being paid for each minute they spent with me, and that if they gave me some time for free, it was subtracted from our time the following week. So how much were their words worth then? And how much was I worth, really?

I often thought of myself as a customer of prostitutes, someone who talked to people, who received human contact from people who did it for money. It was a job, they got paid, and even though it was humiliating, it was still safe. The paid helpers were safe. I never assumed that they liked me or cared about me or that I was worth anything to them, but I never expected to be dismissed or overlooked either. But to walk out into the world again, after so many years, and to believe that people could actually want to be with me for free, and just for fun—that was a massive step. How in the world would I ever believe anything like that? And this dilemma was hard to solve. Because the public employees were precisely that: public employees. And the patient who is there to receive treatment maintains the right to just that, treatment. It can easily become pretty complicated if you bring other things into it, like friendship or private life or other things that may disturb this treatment. However, this doesn't mean that we can't voice the dilemma, as long as it's relevant, and clarify the roles a little bit. "I like you, and if I had met you in another context, I am sure we could have been friends, but right now we can't, as I am required to consider your health and treatment." Or something like that. It doesn't necessarily solve the problem, but then again, the reality is that some problems are hard to solve. We should at least be able to take about them.

Another challenge of walking back into the world is dealing with stigmas and discrimination. You might be exposed to discrimination both from the outside and the inside. Others may look down on you because you are different, but you may also grow so scared of being looked down at that you start seeing things that are not there. In a study conducted by Major and Crooker in 1993, a group of women were made up so that they each looked as though they had a large scar on their face. They could see what they looked like in a mirror first, and then they met another person for a brief conversation. Right before the woman went to meet this other person, the makeup artist asked to add a "protective" layer of moisturizing cream and removed the "scar" without the woman knowing. And then they walked out to have the meeting. Afterward, they were interviewed about the meeting, and despite the fact that none of them had a visible scar—it had been wiped off—many of them described the different kinds of discrimination they had been exposed to, and they even explained what the other person had said or done to make them feel bad. Even though there was no visible scar, the fact that they believed that they had one was enough for them to feel like they were discriminated against. Just like the duckling "knew" that the swans would kill him, and I "knew" that nobody wanted to be with me for free. We can "know" a lot of things, but it doesn't mean that what we know is true.

That doesn't mean that there's not discrimination of patients with psychological conditions. There is. A couple of times I've experienced people treating me badly or unfairly because they knew my past, but that is definitely the exception. When I've told people of my disease, even colleagues, most of them have been nice and professional about it. Some may have been somewhat uncomfortable, embarrassed, or unsure, but they were still nice. When I say that there is still discrimination, I am talking about another, more discreet type of prejudice that doesn't allow me to recover fully. This prejudice usually come in two forms: "You are still sick," and "you were never sick." I don't like either of these assertions. The "you are still sick" variety usually surprises me whenever I encounter it because it often comes from kind, nice people—people I like, and people I like being with. These are people that gladly express that they respect me as a human being and a professional, and that is something I perceive as sincere. And then, suddenly, they will ask what medications I'm on, if I have specific strategies for how to separate hallucinations and real people, or what kind of safety net I have in place for a possible relapse. I have to admit that I can't help laughing when people ask about my trying to live a very organized and structured life. That's not my style. Thinking of myself as an overly structured person seems very alien to me. It is just as crazy when people ask me about medications or hallucinations. I know how I behaved when I was medicated and when I was psychotic, and there is no way I could have functioned in my current life if I were still experiencing these episodes. I wouldn't have managed.

The other side—the "you were never sick" crowd—usually are people who proclaim that I was never really schizophrenic but that I was wrongly diagnosed. To them I say that part of my job today is to diagnose people, and when I compare the criteria for a schizophrenic diagnosis with how I was, both how I remember it and how it is described in my journals, I think the diagnosis fits very well. I would say that the criteria were fulfilled and that the diagnosis was sound. A scientist who is considered as an expert in the field also diagnosed me, and I'm sure he knows the criteria for schizophrenia and the processes for diagnosing it. Still, diagnoses do not fit neatly into natural categories, and there will always be cases of doubt and overlap with other disorders. Of course, my diagnosis could have been wrong, but if so, nobody discovered it until I got better. And that means that there might be people out there who are "wrongly diagnosed" but who haven't discovered this yet. When I was sick, they told me that I was schizophrenic; nobody mentioned the possibility that I was wrongly diagnosed until I was well again. And that's the whole problem. In many instances I have referred to studies showing that about a third of the patients with schizophrenia recover, about one third live well with their symptoms, and about one third will struggle with the symptoms for their entire life. Despite this, schizophrenia is still a box that you can't move in and out of; either you are there forever or you've never been there. This irritates me because it's not true, and because it ensnares people in a life and a label that may hurt them forever.

Life is development. The philosopher Heraklit once said that you can't walk down the same river twice because the next time both you and the river will be different. People must be allowed to develop, to change, and to recover. It is hard enough to do the work without people in the health care system making it even more difficult by saying that it is impossible to get well.

Sometimes people ask me how I am now. "Are you okay?" people say. And I am. Others ask, "Does it ever disappear completely? Is it ever all right again?" That question is more difficult to answer. The disease is gone. I am healthy now, and I am not afraid of being psychotic again. To me, recovering was always a learning process, and it is like other things you learn—like riding a bike or reading. Once you've learned it, it's hard to forget. I don't think I will ever get back to a place where my head is full of shouting voices, where everything is chaos, where my senses are distorted and I don't understand myself or the world. That's over. I understand now. Once you've pulled the beard off Santa Claus and have seen that it's Uncle Arne, it is hard to believe in Santa Claus again. So the disease, for me, is over.

But my story will always be there. I have many scars. On my arms, on my legs, and on my soul. At times it was pretty rough, both what I did to myself and what I was forced to do while under treatment. So there are times that I lie awake at night because of the damage I suffered. Sometimes I have nightmares, although that's rare now. My story still has many holes. If somebody asks me where I was when King Olav died, I have to say that I was sitting in the isolation room, and I never saw the broadcast from the Gulf War. I was at Eidsvoll when Oslo hosted the Winter Olympics, but I was too drugged to remember what happened, and I never traveled up there. These are things I should have known that I don't know because I never experienced them. And there are things I know that maybe I should not have known. Like how it feels to be handcuffed in the back of a car or how wallpaper tastes.

This was never how I planned my life. Some things changed forever, and life took a different direction. I sometimes hear people who have been through a crisis say that now, after it all, they wouldn't be the same without it. I can't say that. I remember how painful it was, how hopeless my life looked. I know I did many stupid things, to myself and to the ones I love. I know how easily everything could have gone wrong. I know that I am incredibly lucky to be alive. So, yes, if I had had the choice, I would have avoided that pain. But I'm sure it's good that I never had the choice. Because I've learned so much that I would have never learned otherwise. Maybe I am a better person for it, and I know that I am a better psychologist. Not because my story is universal and applies to all. But because my experiences have taught me that there is no "they" or "us." We are all just people. We are all different. And we are all basically the same.

So, does it ever disappear completely? I am well today—very well—and I live a good and rich life. Sometimes I am sad. Sometimes I still feel the same vulnerability that I experienced when people categorize me because of a diagnosis I once had and not because of the person I am now. Sometimes I'm hurt and sad because of entirely different reasons. It rains on me as well when it rains, and not all days are good days. But I am healthy. And I often feel the joy of owning my own refrigerator, deciding what I will eat for dinner, and walking out in rain or sunshine whenever I want. I can be tired some mornings, but I am still grateful that I have a job I enjoy. I have exciting work tasks, nice people around me, plans, dreams, and things I enjoy doing. I have a life. And I am well.

Alf Proysen talked about "a day tomorrow" and about starting over "with blank paper and crayons to boot." My paper is not blank. When I was in isolation for ten weeks, the world looked hopeless—ten weeks is a long time in isolation. That's two and a half months, from Christmas to Easter. That's a long time. And even though the nurses sat with me, they did only that—they sat. And they watched. But they weren't allowed to talk to me. Luckily, some rebelled, and they made my life more bearable. But it was still painful. Even in isolation I hurt myself a lot, and to keep me from doing so, they bandaged my hands from the fingers up to my shoulders. At that point I had lost everything even the right to my own fingers, and there was nothing left to take from me. It was utterly hopeless, and I intensely wanted to die because there was no life left to live for. I had no future, and my life was broken. That was when one of the nurses sitting there broke the rule and talked to me. He took a drawing sheet and drew a large square in the middle, then he handed me the sheet along with some crayons and asked me to finish the drawing. My first reaction was to do nothing; I didn't want to expose myself. I wouldn't let him perform a strange experiment on me to find out what hid behind the black square, or something like that. I had lost so much that I had to keep something to myself. But I still took the crayons and started to draw. It was difficult because my hands were covered in bandages, but I did it by holding the crayons between my wrapped palms. And so I filled the sheet with colors. Blood red circles, sheep in gray squares, lonely blue triangles, spring green bubbles, golden half moons. And much more. When I was done, the whole sheet was covered with shapes and colors, and the black square had become part of the pattern. I gave the sheet back to the nurse, he looked at it, and he smiled at me. "I ruined your entire sheet, Arnhild," he said. "I drew a large black square in the middle, which ruined everything, and I drew it with permanent marker so you can't remove it. It is still there, but you created a pattern that included the square. It is not ugly anymore, and it doesn't ruin anything. It has become a natural part of a colorful whole. There is no reason why you can't do the same with your life."

And I did. My sheets are not blank. The square is still there, but it doesn't ruin anything. It is a part of the entirety that is my life. It took time, but I did it. And I used all the colors of the rainbow.

References

Atkinson, R. L., R. C. Atkinson, E. E. Smitm, D. J. Bem, and S. Nolen-Hoeksema. *Hilgard's Introduction to Psychology*. Orlando: Harcourt Brace College Publishers, 1996.

Bentsen, H. *Predictors of expressed emotion in relatives of patients with schizophrenia or related psychoses*. Doktorgrad. Oslo: Medisinsk fakultet, 1998.

Bjerke, André. *Moro-vers*. Oslo, 1982

Brickman, P., V. C. Rabinowitz, J. Karuza, D. Coates, E. Cohn, and L. Kidder. "Models of helping and coping." *American Psychologist: Journal of the American Psychological Association*, 37 (4), 1982: 368-384.

Dahl, A. A., L. Eitinger, U. F. Malt, and N. Retterstøl. *Lærebok i psykiatri*. Oslo: Universitetsforlaget. Glass og Singer, 2000.

Dahl, A., et.al. *Lærebok i psykiatri*. Oslo: Universitetsforlaget, 1994.

Green, Hannah. *Jeg lovet deg aldri en rosenhage*, Norwegian transl. Tone Bull, Oslo, 1964, 1971.

Knardahl, S. *Kropp og sjel. Psykologi, biologi og helse*. Oslo: Universitetsforlaget, 1998.

Lagerlöf, Selma. "Keiserinnens skattkiste." *Legender og histo-rier*, Norwegian transl. Finn Halvorsen, Oslo, 1960.

Major, B. and J. Crocker. "Social stigma." Edited by I. D. M. Mackie and D.L. Hamilton. *Affect, cognition, and stereotyping.* (s. 345–368). San Diego: Academic press, 1993.

Markus, H. and A. Ruvolo. "Possible Selves: Personalized Representations of Goals." Edited by I. Pervin, L.A. *Goal Concepts in Personality and Social Psychology.* New Jersey: Lawrence Erlbaum Associates, Publishers, 1989.

Scott, R. A. *The Making of Blind Men. A Study of Adult Socialization.* New Brunswick: Transaction Books, 1981.

ALSO AVAILABLE

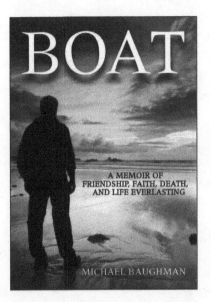

When ten-year-old Michael Baughman moves to Hawaii with his parents, he is troubled and confused. His father doesn't provide the guidance Baughman needs and the boy doesn't know who to turn to. When a larger-than-life Hawaiian "beachboy" named Boat takes Baughman under his wing, the boy finds a teacher and mentor. Boat is 285 pounds of solid muscle but gentle spirituality, and he introduces the boy to the ways of Hawaiian mysticism, offering simple, profound wisdom that helps Baughman thrive in an otherwise lonely childhood. Even after Baughman leaves the islands seven years later, the unlikely friendship endures for the rest of Boat's life, influencing and inspiring the author to this day.

Baughman's narrative begins with a distressed boy at a Pittsburgh Pirates baseball game and ends more than six decades later with himself as a content old man experiencing a miracle in Mexico. With a photographic memory, Baughman recalls virtually verbatim every significant conversation he had with Boat. Boat spoke Hawaiian Pidgin English, and its unique lilt and rhythm grace this touching memoir. A testament to friendship and the revelations provoked by wisdom in unexpected places.

US $16.95 hardcover ISBN: 978-1-61145-493-2

ALSO AVAILABLE

A Memoir of Love and Loss

Tanya Chernov

A Real Emotional Girl tells the true story of young Tanya, growing up in the wonderland of her family's summer camp. At sixteen, this idyllic life is interrupted when she must face her father's sudden illness. Tanya, her mother, and two brothers find themselves cramped in a tiny cabin in a tiny town in northern Wisconsin in the dead of winter. There they wait for her father to die of cancer. Separated from friends and civilization, Tanya has only her fears and uncertainty for company.

At the age of twenty, Tanya loses a man who was not only her father but a surrogate father to thousands. Richard Chernov was a man who shared himself, humor and all, with just about everyone who would let him. And with this same unflagging commitment and passion, Tanya shares her struggles and the blessings she finds in them. Her memoir is a complex amalgam of human strength and fragility, which creates an inimitable coming-of-age story. This is a story of family and pain, of survival and growing up, and ultimately of love. For anyone who has ever experienced loss, *A Real Emotional Girl* offers a glimpse, provocative in its raw honesty, into the nature of grief and the positive transformation that can follow.

US $24.95 hardcover ISBN: 978-1-61608-869-9

ALSO AVAILABLE

"Dr. Spock? Check. Penelope Ann Leach (remember her?)? Check. *What to Expect When You're Expecting*? Check. I had a seven hundred dollar Bellini crib for God's sake! I was perfect. And so was Mia when she was born . . ."

So begins Kim Stagliano's electrifying and hilarious memoir of her family's journey raising three daughters with autism. In these stories, Stagliano has joined the ranks of David Sedaris and Augusten Burroughs with her amazing ability to lay everything on the table—from family, friends, and enemies to basement floods to birthdays to (possible) heroin addictions—eviscerating and celebrating the absurd. From her love of Howard Stern to her increasing activism in the autism community and exhaustive search for treatments that will help her daughters, she covers it all. Always outspoken, often touching, and sometimes heartbreaking, Kim Stagliano is a powerful new voice in comedic writing—her "Kimoir" (as she calls it) will be a must-read within the autism community and the literary world at large.

US $14.95 paperback ISBN: 978-1-61608-459-2

ALSO AVAILABLE

Jeni Decker is five-foot nothing and one hundred and [redacted] pounds—a self described roly-poly, forty-something, Reubenesque bon-bon of a gal, often called cute but never sexy. She has two sons with autism on opposite ends of the spectrum (Jake and Jaxson), a husband who prefers hunting to household chores, an Australian Shepherd named Sugar, and an albino frog named Humbert Humbert. This is her story—a brash, personal, and sometimes shocking memoir of one woman's determination to raise two healthy kids with autism and keep her sanity in the process. It's not always easy. Between "poop" incidents, temper tantrums, and the "helpful" advice about parenting from her fellow citizens in the grocery store, Jeni often finds herself wanting to throw something. With chapters like: "Tickling the Weiner," "Why I Hate Pokemon," "Santa: Give it a Friggin' Rest, Already," and "Oprah's the Reason My Kid Thinks I Want to Drown Him in the Tub," *I Wish I Were Engulfed in Flames* also includes mini-chapters written by her eldest son, Jake.

Readers looking for laughter and inspiration will find it here aplenty, along with tons of surreal anecdotes that will have you either shaking your head in disbelief (for those unacquainted with the world of autism) or nodding with recognition (for those who are). As Jeni says, "I developed a new 'normal.'"

US $24.95 hardcover ISBN: 978-1-61608-485-1